W8-BWR-571

...P INTO ADVENTURE WITH A TIGER IN THE TANK WITH—

...RY RHODAN—The #1 Man of 2042.

...nald Bell—Perry's No. 1 Friend.

...n D. Mercant—Solar Defense Marshal.

...g—A navigational mathematician.

...rag, Miltau, Sgts. Brack & Fip—Terranians assisting Perry ...dan.

Lts. S. Seegers & Peter H. Hasting—Crewmen of the *Tigris*.

Kitai Ishibashi—A tall slender intellectual Oriental mutant with super powers of suggestion.

The Robot Regent—The Positronicon on Arkon 3 that is the absolute ruler of the Great Imperium.

Fellmer Lloyd—This member of Rhodan's Mutant Corps perceives & analyzes brainwaves.

Tako Kakuta—Mutant of Japanese ancestry with teleportational ability.

Alf Renning—You must discover his identity for yourself.

Gen. Sutokk—Commander of the Arkonide fleet stationed on Ekhas.

Thur-Ges—An officer in the spacefleet of the Regent of Arkon.

EKHONIDES

Egg-or—Head of planetary defense for the planet Ekhas.

Exwin—Chief of traffic control at the Ent-than spaceport.

Sassas—An expert on positronicons.

Do-Man—Egg-or's Chief of Police.

Ulgald—An engineer.

En-E—A Colleague of Egg-or, stationed on the planet Soral.

And the spaceships *Tigris, Lotus, Mab 1, Ebneb, Orinoco, Oak-Oak* & *Eugenio*.

PERRY RHODAN: Peacelord of the Universe

Series and characters created and directed by Karl-Herbert Scheer and Walter Ernsting.

ACE BOOKS EDITION

Managing Editor: Forrest J Ackerman

Translator: Wendayne Ackerman

Art Director: Charles Volpe

Editor: Pat LoBrutto

Fellmer Lloyd

Perry

63

THE TIGRIS LEAPS

by

Kurt Brand

ace books

A Division of Charter Communications Inc.
1120 Avenue of the Americas
New York, N.Y. 10036

THE *TIGRIS* LEAPS

DEDICATION

This American Edition

Dedicated to

TIGRINA,

The Original Tiger Girl

and SF Fanne Still Purring Along.

ORDER OF THE ACTION

RHOFANS!

Your suggestions, complaints & ideas have not gone to waste.

At the end of August, just before the fantastic World Science Fiction Convention attended by 4500 sf fans, including the Ackerman & Ackerwoman, a historic event for Perry in America took place in the offices of Ace Books in New York City. PR fans from all corners of the state came to discuss the Peacelord's future.

We were all ushered down a corridor with offices filled with books on either side. When we finally reached our destination we saw none other than Forrest J and Wendayne Ackerman waiting to greet us. All the way from California for the occasion!

During the course of the meeting, presided over by the president & vice-president of the company, we saw & discussed many different things.

We had the privilege of seeing German PERRY RHODANS.

A PERRY RHODAN dictionary.

A book of PR spaceship blueprints.

And 3 other series which are offshoots of PR. There is, as we all know by now, ATLAN; a new one (to us) called DRAGON—a sword & sorcery magazine about the descendants of Atlantis; plus, one more called The Planet Series—involving all the characters of regular PR but the story centers around a different one each time. The first, "The Center of the Galaxy", will probably be published in hardcover form.

We discussed PERRY four-a-month . . . binders for our collections of PR . . . posters of Perry, Pucky, Khrest, Thora, et al . . . "T" (for Thora) shirts and "P" shirts for Perry fans.

We saw some original Gray Morrow paintings which were nothing short of fantastic.

We heard exciting news about TV possibilities for a PR series.

To wrap up this already exciting day, Forry & Wendayne autographed PR numbers 53 & 54, magabooks from the "future" which had not yet had public release at that time.

Believe me—and I'm sure I speak for all present, which included one young lady & her father who was also a PR fan—this was a memorable event I will not soon, correction, not ever forget.

Perry truly yours,

MIKE FEIGIN

1/ THE DEVASTATING DIAGRAM

THEY'D DONE IT!

3 men with exhausted faces sighed deeply as their department's computer spewed out a length of tape with an audible click. The tape fell rustling into a cup-shaped receptacle and at the same time the computer, a device based on positronic principles, shut off and the humming and vibrating died away. A penetrating silence suddenly reigned in the room.

Chief logician Nourag got up and crossed to the machine, taking the computer tape from its receptacle. Then he turned and looked triumphantly at his 2 colleagues.

It was the finest reward for a work that had occupied them for 36 hours.

36 hours before, Chief Logician Nourag had been summoned to Allan D. Mercant, Marshal of Solar Defense.

"I need," Mercant had said, "in 40 hours, a set of precise coordinates according to which our solar system would appear to be in the following position . . . take this down if you will, Nourag . . . Phi 16 degrees, 34 minutes, 22 seconds; Psi 03:05:45; and Chi 44:43:01. Your range will be between 3500 & 4200 light-years from Earth. No more, no less. Within those limits, where you go is up to you and your men to decide.

"Once you've determined those coordinates, you will have the interesting task of calculating the distance from the Earth's fictitious location to those star systems known to us.

"To put it simply, your mission is this: supply me data in the next 40 years that would guarantee that a spaceship of our fleet using it would never find its way back to Earth. However, the data must appear utterly genuine and stand up to the most suspicious examination without evidencing any hint of deliberate foul play."

With that the chief logician had been dismissed.

And now they had done it: in 36 hours, on the 4th runthrough. 3 times before the positronicon had stopped during the middle of computations. The data it had been fed was not sufficient to reach any conclusions but Nourag and his colleagues were able to determine readily enough what information was lacking and supply it.

Nourag, a small, slender man, was radiant with joy now. The long plastic tape with its encoded symbols was like an open book in his mother language to him.

"Miltau," he said to his closest co-worker, "call Marshall Mercant and tell him our job is finished—and so is our strength, for that matter."

But the Solar Defense Marshall could not be reached.

"Alright," said Nourag, "then I'll wait for him. Thank you, gentlemen. You can go now."

Nourag had been alone for only a few minutes when he had a visit from Esting, the navigational mathematician.

Esting fell tiredly into a seat. "That Solar Defense bunch," he moaned. "One of these days they're going to kill us all. I had to calculate spring coordinates . . . Good Lord! I'd hate to be flying in the spaceship going into transition with *my* data! What in heaven's name is all this nonsense for, anyway?"

But it was not nonsense at all.

In all details, it was a very carefully thought-out plan.

For 2 hours Perry Rhodan, Reginald Bell, Marshall Mercant and Maj. Clyde Ostal of the Solar Security Service had been sitting at the final conference.

Allan D. Mercant handed new reports to Perry Rhodan, Administrator of the Solar Imperium. Rhodan skimmed over them and nodded. "The picture is becoming more complete," he said, "but we've waited long enough. The reports from our agents are growing steadily sparser and less detailed. Our experience with the Robot Regent indicates that that means Arkon is attempting to double-cross us again." He laid his hand on the reports that Mercant had given him. "Here we see how strong the probability is that Arkon has begun development of its new compensator-detector. Mercant, not even you know how dangerous our situation has become in the last 3 days!"

The Defense Marshall looked at Rhodan in astonishment. Rhodan reached behind himself and produced a slip of paper on which a diagram had been drawn. He laid it out on the table.

Bell, Mercant and Maj. Ostal bent over the diagram in curiosity.

The diagram came from the space freighter *Orinoco* and was 3 days old.

2 days before, the *Orinoco* had returned from a freight run to the M-13 System, landing at Terrania a full 6 hours behind schedule.

The 6-hour delay was due to unplanned transitions. The commander of the *Orinoco* fortunately belonged to the officers of the Terran spacefleet and merchant marine and consequently took his work very seriously.

The diagram that now disturbed 3 of the men taking

part in the conference had deeply shaken him as well. And thus 30 minutes after his arrival in Terrania, he had requested to speak with Perry Rhodan.

"This is too much!" Bell exclaimed, wiping the sweat from his forehead.

Mercant's eyes shimmered dangerously.

Maj. Clyde Ostal had gone pale.

The testimony of the diagram was devastating.

Mercant began to speak, as though lecturing a class. He rarely spoke in that tone: only when he had been deeply disturbed. His pen flew over the diagram, pointing various things out. "Here . . . that's the *Orinoco's* transition . . . uninteresting. But here, at 0434:05 hours, ship's time, the vessel came out of hyperspace. And there . . ." Mercant's hand trembled. ". . . At 0435:36 hours, ship's time, just 1 minutes & 31 seconds later, the first Arkonidean ship flew towards it. And that 1.23 light-years from where the *Orinoco* was going to land.

"No sir, I didn't know that. That's the catastrophe we've been trying to prevent for more than half a century. And tomorrow or the day after tomorrow, the first Arkonide *Titan*-type spacespheres will be landing here by the hundreds!"

It was astounding that Bell did not comment at first. This was something quite out of character for him. He, a man whose bent for flying off the handle at the least provocation was well-known throughout the Solar Imperium, merely ran both hands through his reddish hair while gasping loudly for breath. Finally he burst out with: "What a fine fishket! * The Druufs to the right of us, the double-crossing Robot Brain to the left of us . . . and the Positronic scrap pile knows the position of the Earth now . . .!"

* 21st century expression for "kettle of fish"

"I don't believe it knows yet," Rhodan interrupted. "The range of the Arkonide structural compensators is *still* limited." He reached behind himself again and laid the 2d diagram on the table. "Commodore Lyst of the *Orinoco* had the fortunate idea of testing the capabilities of the new Arkonide device with a spring near M-13. This diagram doesn't tell us why the Arkonide sensor can't pick up the frequency of our structural compensators from a distance of more than 10 light-years but it does tell us that we Terrans don't dare lose another minute . . ." He allowed a pause to emphasize what he had yet to say. ". . . And we have to first make arrangements so that all our spacers can return to Earth when we transmit a coded message for them to do so; but making at least 20 different transitions while on their way before they finally set course for Terra on their last spring. That, gentlemen, is our situation at the presentime."

"As if that motorized bucket of bolts hasn't given us enough trouble already!" Bell cried out angrily. "Perry, don't you feel an urge to send Pucky to the Robot Regent so our little friend can 'play' with him a bit?"

In spite of the earnest situation, Perry Rhodan could not repress a smile. Bell's suggestion of sending the telepathic, telekinetic and teleportative mousebeaver extraordinary, Pucky, to face the giant computer on Arkon 3 was no joke but just the thought of a *playing* Pucky was enough to cause a smile.

Had he been given such a mission, Pucky would have certainly displayed his single incisor tooth, as he always did to express his joy. Teleporting himself inside the mammoth positronicomputer and then beginning to "play"—destroying the positronicon section by section with his telekinetic powers unleased full-force—would have been his idea of fun.

However . . .

"Such a suicide mission is out of the question for Pucky," Rhodan said, tabling the idea. "Mercant, don't have your agents concentrating their attention on the construction of the Arkonide sensing equipment. I'd much rather know if they're started mass production of the device. Its construction is less important . . ."

Bell stared at his friend, startled. Rhodan overlooked it, turning to Maj. Ostal. "Are you ready enough that you could take off at 1245 hours?"

Mercant answered for Ostal. "They'll be ready by then, sir. The extra equipment is ready now and the rest of the work is just routine."

Rhodan turned to his friend. "Reggie, I asked you to have the light cruiser *Lotus* refitted. How has the work been going?"

"*We're* ready," he replied, gesturing angrily, "but those pickle people, the Swoons, seem like *they* never will be. If I could only see *what* they're trying to do. These microscopically small devices of theirs are beginning to get on my nerves."

"They'd get on my nerves, too, Reggie . . . if the Swoons were working for Arkon instead of us." That was all Rhodan had to say about that but for Bell those words had their own meaning. He knew Perry Rhodan better than anyone else and he was aware that when Rhodan spoke in such riddles, something was up and would soon reveal itself, usually at some unexpected moment.

"Anything else, gentlemen?" Rhodan looked at the men questioningly.

"Yes sir," said Maj. Ostal. "Is our destination still the star system of Naral?"

"Yes it is. According to the latest reports of our agents, suspicion has increased that one or even several compensator-sensors are on the planet Ekhas, possibly built into Arkonide ships. We know already through the commodore of the *Orinoco* which Arkonide planet is definitely the site of a sensor unit but re-programming your ship's extra equipment would cause us to lose 5 days—and that much time, gentlemen, we don't have. In the next few days or hours Arkon could succeed in increasing the range of their compensator sensor to a thousand or more light-years. What then?"

"I *still* like the idea of sending Pucky to pay a call on the Robot Brain!" Bell muttered, vexed.

Perry Rhodan replied without hesitation. "We need both Pucky and the Positronicon on Arkon 3—we can't afford to lose *either* of them!"

10 ADVENTURES FROM NOW
You'll board the
Spaceship of Ancestors

2/ PRISONERS: ENT-THAN

With the take-off of the spherical freighter *Tigris*, which measured 100 meters in diameter, at precisely 1245 hours from the spaceport at Terrania, an operation began with the precision of an adding machine—an operation that the Solar Imperium had to carry through to a successful conclusion at all costs.

Commander of the ship was Maj. Clyde Ostal of the Solar Security Service. The crew was 32 men recruited from Allan D. Mercant's Defense Ministry.

They knew what was at stake. They also knew that their mission was dangerous. Even though the star system of Naral was "only" 4536 light-years from Earth and from Arkon 1, 2 & 3 around 34000, it belonged nonetheless to the Great Imperium, for the people who lived there were Arkonide descendants and had never forgotten that they were Arkonides. Their loyalty to the Imperium was proverbial; their contacts with Arkon 3 were so close they could not be any closer.

Speeding along at 85% SPEOL, the *Tigris* shot through the solar system, passed at length the relay station on Pluto and then plunged into the gulf between the stars.

Rarely had a ship been sent out from Earth with such precise orders as the *Tigris*, which was clearly identifiable as a Terran trade vessel.

The vast storerooms were filled to the limits with goods that were already impatiently awaited in the Tatlira system. Hypercom messages from Terran space freighters to Terran trade offices on alien worlds—inquiries and messages for relay between solar freighters underway—all these had been inconspicuously in progress for 3 days and whoever was listening in from the "other" side saw in the last transmission of the freighter *Eugenio*, which stated that the *Tigris* would arrive on 18 June 2042, only a typical commercial message.

"Listening in" on hypercom traffic was as common as ever. The Galactic Traders listened in on all frequencies with a thousand ears. Arkon listened in from Globular Cluster M-13 or from its advanced bases on various worlds. And the Solar Imperium listened too. No one, it seemed, wanted to be caught unawares by some new development.

Maj. Clyde Ostal grinned as he listened to the last hypercom message of the *Eugenio*.

With that, Order 17 was carried out. Now he could go on to the next.

Order 18 read: Undertake Transition 1 & 2 only with the extra device. Shut off ship's Positronicon. Shut off data & storage banks. Check out 3 times! Inspecting equipment at 10 minute intervals:

Maj. Clyde Ostal

Lt. S. Seegers

Lt. Peter H. Hasting

The "extra device" had been specially constructed for the 2 first transitions of the *Tigris* and in reality was nothing more than a small positronicon. It had been programmed to carry the trade vessel safely through 2 hytrans from one determined point in space to another 1375 light-years away.

The small crew of the spacesphere experienced the unpleasant shock of transition twice. As the last man in the control room recovered, they all looked to the panorama screen, which offered them a view of an alien sky.

The extra device went into action once more. Within a few seconds it had calculated the coordinates of the trade vessel's new position to the 5th decimal place and, comparing the result with Order 19, Maj. Ostal found the two in agreement.

Now Order 20 waited to be carried out.

In Cabin 8, the alarm clock rang out in 2 short bursts, then 1 long. 4 men had been waiting for the signal. They hurriedly left their cabin and headed for the control room. There they wordlessly began the work of detaching the heavy extra device from the ship's up-to-now idle positronicon and removing all traces of any evidence that an auxiliary unit had ever been coupled to it.

They were still busy with the last of the labor when a work robot lumbered in and waited for orders to carry the extra device away.

Its steel limbs did not even strain as it lifted the unit, which weighed at least 150 kilos, and left the control room with it.

The robot was expected at Hatch B. The inner hatch door opened up, the robot stepped into the airlock and then the door closed behind it again.

Maj. Clyde Ostal and 3 officers watched the panorama screen. Suddenly a square object appeared on it, floating through space past the ship—the extra device which the work robot had thrown out.

During the next few minutes Ostal turned off one *Tigris* defense field after another. The extra device floated farther and farther away at a constant speed.

Lt. S. Seegers switched on his microphone and called the disintegrator crew. "Open fire on floating object!"

3 seconds later all men in the control room had to briefly shut their eyes to avoid being blinded by the

sudden glare on the screen. The extra device had vanished in a cascade of rapid atomic destruction.

Nothing more remained to hint that the *Tigris* had come to this point in space with the help of a rather expensive technical trick.

Order 21, the next to last, remained now.

Maj. Clyde Ostal called up the Com Center of his ship. "Contact our settlement on Goszul's Planet in the Tatlira System and tell our people there that in 3 hours & 10 minutes the freighter *Tigris* out of Terrania will be landing. Transmit the message over the scrambler and use the normal merchant code. Over."

The Solar Imperium had known for some weeks that the Springers could now not only decipher the Terran merchant code but also reconstruct scrambled messages.

"Lt. Hasting?" Maj. Clyde Ostal turned and gave him the list of orders 1 thru 22. "Annihilation of the equipment as ordered. You'll be responsible to me if even some ashes are left over!"

Clyde Ostal's face, which usually was inflexible and displayed no feelings, was now open and expressive. He, the 45-year-old commander of the operation, was letting his men perceive that they were nearing a decisive point.

"Transition to the Tatlira System!" he ordered. But a mocking smile suddenly played around his mouth. Over on his right, 2 officers were feeding the ship's positronicon the new data. Not only the coordinates of the ship's current position were necessary to insure a flawless transition but also the energy values calculated by the positronicon as being essential for reaching Tatlira by way of hyperspace. Hyperspace, of course, was that "in-between" space which could be comprehended only mathematically.

Although the huge computer aboard the *Tigris* had been completely misprogrammed by Earthly scientists after hours of team effort, it operated in spite of the falsified data just as Marshall Mercant and the scientists had hoped it would.

Daring a hypertrans with utterly garbled programming and maybe 1/10th of correct data, and still feeling confident of coming out alright even in "the wrong place in space", was not simply light-headed recklessness on the part of the *Tigris*' crew. They were confident that the scientists on Perry Rhodan's staff had known what they were doing.

"Transition in 10 minutes!" announced the vocoder of the positronicon chronometer, then began the countdown.

At X minus 5 minutes, Clyde Ostal called up the Com Center again. "All clear . . . is the message ready to send in the automatic transmitter? Are the scrambler and distorter units ready to go?"

"Yes, Major. The text of the message is uncoded, as ordered!" The officer on duty at the transmitter wanted to emphasize once more that the procedure was an unusual one. Uncoded hypercom messages were a rarity.

The last machinery in the transition sequence switched on. All the energy stations were in operation as well as all the transformers. On the control panel in front of Ostal one instrument light after another lit up in bright green, signifying "Go". The major did not concentrate unduly on what was happening before him: Arkonide hypnotraining had so ingrained the intricacies of piloting a starship in him that he was hardly capable of a wrong move.

X minus 1 . . .

At zero the *Tigris* sliced into hyperspace in a burst of unimaginable energy.

The image on the vidscreen of 10,000 near & far stars shining coldly in the void seemed to fly apart—and every man on board the spacesphere ceased to exist, as well. Although hyperspace did not take a man's life away from him, it did take away the usual form of his existence.

And then it was all over. The transition had taken place in an amount of time that could not even be measured as time because during that "time" it had been in a continuum where the factor of "time" had no validity.

Moaning, the 33 men who had sprung with the *Tigris* tried to recover from the shock of transition. Fortunately the effects of the shock were shortlived and the reality of their new situation forced them to their senses with a jolt.

Not one light-hour away, directly in the ship's path, shone a small, yellowish star. The Terran freighter continued towards it at a velocity 90% of light.

Every officer in the control room was feverish with tension. Everyone knew that the *Tigris* had not emerged from hyperspace in the Tatlira System but rather in the Naral System, 4536 light-years from Earth.

The 3d planet, Ekhas, the only one of altogether 8 planets which was inhabited, was their destination.

The energy stations, energy storage banks, transitional forcefields and the transformers, all shut down one by one. Finally the structocomp, which had brought the merchant ship through a leap of more than 4500 light-years turned off.

In the control room a new counting-off had begun, announcing without interruption the time that had elapsed since the re-emergence of the *Tigris* into normal space.

2 men sat at the radarscope, concentrating their entire attention on the equipment.

"3 minutes & 1 second," announced the posichron.*

No human in the control room spoke. No calls came in over the intercom. Each of the 33 men aboard knew that the first 10 minutes after leaving hyperspace could be of decisive importance.

"4 minutes & 30 seconds," droned the chronometer.

At 4 minutes & 38 seconds, Lt. Manteau called from the radarscope. "Our ship's been spotted—we're right in the middle of a radar beam!"

The officer in the Com Center had been listening over the intercom, as he had been instructed. In the next moment he sent off a hypercom message by way of the scrambler.

The message was short, consisting of only 2 words: "Ship spotted". The scrambler had compressed those 2 words into an impulse 1/5000th of their original length. The officer sending out the message tried to make out the typical curve the 2 words would make on the oscilligraph but he was not even able to see a momentary flash.

The Com officer rubbed his hands together in satisfaction. Everything in his department had gone smoothly. He just hoped everything else would go equally well.

3 sizeable structural shocks were registered in the immediate area by the *Tigris*. A few minutes later 3 tiny points weakly reflecting the light of Naral appeared on the screen, evidently coming from the nearby star system.

Maj. Ostal called the Com Center on his microphone. "Have they hailed us yet?"

"No, Major."

* Positronichronometer

"Then try to call them on the Arkonide trade-frequency. The usual message, you know . . ."

The com officer acted immediately. Broadcasting in Interkosmo, he announced the ship's name, class, home port, destination and so forth. As destination he gave the Tatlira system, giving the impression that the crew of the *Tigris* did not know they were *not* in the Tatlira system.

Now he was nothing more than a crew member of a harmless Terran freighter—certainly not a trained agent of Solar Defense. He did not find the role hard to play and when the demand came thundering from 1 of the 3 oncoming spacers for the *Tigris* to reduce its speed, he began to stutter over the radio so well, and to choose his words so appropriately for the situation, that his colleague with silent gestures ordered him to get his play-acting over with as fast as possible.

In the control room the loudspeaker carried both query and reply. Maj. Clyde Ostal's amusement showed on his face. It was good that no one aboard the 3 Arkonide battlespacers could see him at this moment.

"Yes sir, Commander . . . Radio silence, complete radio silence. But if I may ask . . ."

The com officer of the *Tigris* could not ask.

The commander of the Arkonide battleships was a rabid fighter over the radio, threatening attack with all weapons and total destruction of the Terran merchant vessel.

Maj. Ostal then ordered the com officer: "Put me on the transmission!"

The screen in front of him flickered and then formed the image of a grim-looking Arkonide commander.

"Clyde Ostal, Captain of the merchant ship *Tigris* . . ." Ostal began.

The arrogant-looking Arkonide made an imperious gesture. "Turn off your defense screens. I'm bringing my ship alongside. As soon as you observe that a boarding party wishes to enter your ship you are to open the main hatch. End of transmission!"

With that the first conversation between the three 300-meter Arkonide spacespheres and the small *Tigris* was at an end.

"Alright," said Ostal calmly, "these gentlemen are going to have their way!" But a slight undertone in his voice promised nothing pleasant. Then, over the connection to the Com Center, the Major asked: "Have you been listening in? If yes, then don't make any permanent recordings of the conversation we just had, and erase temporary tapes. I want the Arkonides to think we're really stupid."

"1 of the 3 ships is transmitting on the Robot Brain's frequency, Major. The text of the message has been coded, scrambled and speeded up. The connection has been in existence ever since I told them our destination was the Tatlira System."

Ostal smiled wanly. The Arkonides had fallen for the ruse immediately but it bothered him that they would act so hostile towards a Terran spaceship.

Perry Rhodan and the Robot Brain were officially still allies.

Lt. Peter H. Hasting reported quietly. "The boarding party is floating towards us. They're bringing battle robots with them!"

"The way things have been going, I'm not surprised." Ostal was not to be shaken out of his calm. If this new development had not been anticipated, either, by the same token it would not prevent him from carrying out the mission Perry Rhodan had given him.

An unruffled and unshocked security officer called in from the main hatch. "10 Arkonides and 15 battle robots on board, sir!"

At the same moment a report came in from the Com Center: "The exchange on the Robot Regent wavelength had just terminated. The length of the discussion was 14 minutes!"

Clyde Ostal glanced meaningfully at Hasting. The young lieutenant, who had already proved himself in a number of dangerous missions, nodded slightly from his post at the positronicon. He quietly rested his hand on the *Erase* switch that was connected to the *Spring Coordinate* section of the memory banks. However, the officers in the control room well knew that pulling the Erase switch would not completely destroy that important data within t e positronicon as a whole. Despite the erasure of the central storage bank, the hytrans coordinates could be calculated with data taken from other memory centers—but the work would take a goodly amount of time.

The heavy control room door opened automatically.

Lt. Hasting of the Solar Defense, now posing as a merchant marine with the rank of lieutenant aboard the *Tigris*, calmly pulled the Erase switch. A yellow light flickered brightly, impossible to overlook.

"Halt! Let that go!" shouted the first Arkonide to enter the control room, seeing what Hasting was doing.

"Alright," said Hasting, stepping back from the positronicon control panel. He smiled ironically. "But you're a little late!"

A minute later all the officers in the control room and the Com Center were out of work. They had been crowded into a corner and guarded by battle robots while the Arkonides took over the *Tigris*.

The Arkonide officer whose face Ostal had already seen on the vidscreen suddenly asked: "Who is the captain here?"

Clyde Ostal stepped forward. "I am."

"Did you give an order to erase the hytrans coordinates?"

"Of course!" Ostal yelled angrily, finding he did not have to play-act his rage now. "You were acting like pirates, not Arkonides!"

"We are Ekhonides, Terran, and I am commander of the Arkonide battlefleet stationed on Ekhas." If the Ekhonide, a tall proud man who looked about 40 in Terran years, had hoped to make an impression with his statement, he was disappointed.

"And we are Terrans, Ekhonide, and I'm a captain of Perry Rhodan's! Perry Rhodan will issue a protest to the Robot Regent on Arkon 3 and you will have to answer to the Regent personally for boarding a Terran vessel with engine trouble in such a high-handed fashion!"

Another Ekhonide came out of the Com Center and whispered a few words to his commander, who grinned approvingly and looked back at Clyde Ostal, even more arrogant than before.

"Weren't you on your way to the Tatlira System, Terran?" he asked mockingly.

Ostal played the unsuspecting innocent. "I don't understand this at all. Where do you get the nerve and the impudence to operate with your battlefleet right in front of Goszul's Planet? You're Ekhonides, you say? Ekhonides . . . ? But the Ekhonides inhabit the 3d planet of the Naral System and . . ."

"That is correct!" the overbearing commander interrupted. "That's why your Perry Rhodan doesn't interest us in the least! Because you are *not* in the Tatlira System—your misspring brought you all the way into the Naral System. Do you think your Rhodan would look for you *here?* We Ekhonides don't think so. Now go back with your men!"

Wordlessly, Clyde Ostal followed the order. He did not concern himself over the tight, bitter faces of his men. They were playing their parts just as much as he was playing his.

Then they watched unconcerned as 5 Ekhonides put the *Tigris* back on course. 1 of the 5 turned out to be familiar with the English language and knew all the written and spoken terms having to do with spaceflight.

Terran spaceships, in principle modelled after Arkonide spacers, had retained the practical spherical form. When, 2 hours of flying time later, the *Tigris* landed along with the 3 ships of the Arkonide fleet at the Ent-Thans spaceport, it looked as though a mixed squadron were returning from a patrol flight.

Maj. Clyde Ostal and his officers had seen on the panorama screen what a large city Ent-Than was and that on the spaceport field, which curved half-way around the city boundary like a vast crescent, ships were taking off and landing continuously.

Then after landing, the 33 Terrans were marched across the giant spaceport plaza. Naral, listed on the charts as a small yellow star, seemed from the surface of the planet Ekhas just as large as the Earth's own sun.

A cloudless blue sky vaulted over this world, which had been settled by Arkonides for more than 10,000 years. If during the passage of millenniums they had become also known as Ekhonides, they had remained Arkonides at heart—but healthy and enterprising Arkonides.

The Terrans were marched for a distance of 5 kilometers. For over an hour they had to endure scornful looks, mocking remarks and undisguised contempt.

As they came to the spaceport's huge reception and administration building, they were crammed into a vehicle designed to carry just 15 men.

Clyde Ostal protested. An Ekhonide with an unknown rank insignia on his chest listened to Ostal's protest with an expression of arrogant scorn on his face, then asked contemptuously: "So what do you want me to do about it? You're nothing but a Terran."

Maj. Clyde Ostal felt the blood rushing into his face but he controlled himself. He drew his head back and said calmly in the most fluent Arkonese: "How right you are, Ekhonide! I'm a Terran, not a degenerate Arkonide or arrogant Ekhonide, and for that I thank all my lucky stars!"

Ostal turned abruptly around and left the confused Ekhonide little suspecting he would see him again the next day, and pressed himself in with his 32 men in the transport vehicle.

Guard vehicles studded with weaponry accompanied the transport on both sides. Escape was impossible. The Terrans were taken deeper & deeper into the sea of houses of Ent-Than. The column finally drew up in front of a huge skyscraper hotel. Star Of Arkon read the sign in Arkonese.

But the hotel had a shady side. 1/5th of the giant building, that portion 800 meters high, was a prison.

A special antigravity lift brought them up to a point 3 feet in front of a transparent barrier of forcefields. Lt. Hasting did not understand the warning a robot gave him and fell against the forcefield, breaking his arm.

He was immediately separated from his comrades. Then the barrier disappeared and the 32 remaining members of the *Tigris* crew were marched into the prison of Ent-Than.

25 ADVENTURES FROM NOW
You'll be puzzled by
The Mystery of the Anti

3/ PROSPECT: BRAINLASH

Even as the crew of the *Tigris* was still on the way to the prison, which like the hotel in the same building bore the name Star of Arkon, the planetary security service of Ekhas had taken 2 dozen of its best specialists off their jobs and brought them to the Terran spaceship.

There, these men met 3 communications scientists.

The specialists assigned to the hypercom equipment of the *Tigris* were instructed to carry out their investigations with all possible care and accuracy for they were to determine whether or not the *Tigris* had been able to transmit a call for help to its home solar system which eluded Ekhonide surveillance of the hypercom frequencies.

In the control room, 8 specialists busied themselves with the ship's positronicon while others examined the controls of the structural compensator. The latter group then proceeded to that part of the ship where the actual structocomp machinery itself stood, that huge device which up to now had prevented springs through hyperspace from being detected and measured.

Even the radar was not ignored: the remaining 2 Ekhonides of the 2 dozen, however, went through the paperwork. They studied the shipping manifests and the waybills and went carefully over the flight orders. The English language and its specialized terms were no problem to them: hypnotraining had allowed them to learn this language as well as their mother tongue.

The 3 Ekhonides detailed to inspect the Terran ship's

engines quickly finished their work and reported back to Egg-or, who was leading the operation himself.

"The engines operated without any trouble, Lord. There must be another reason for the misspring. We've also looked over the ship's energy reservoirs: there's enough energy on hand for 100 hytrans. That's not even taking into consideration the potential of the generators, which by the way are superior to those of Arkonide construction—better, more powerful, yet fundamentally simpler. We——"

Egg-or, the Ekhonide to whom Maj. Ostal had protested at the vast spaceport administration building about the undignified treatment accorded his men, gestured for silence. "Save your explanations and findings for the written report—and don't forget to make it in octuplicate. Thank you."

Then his pocket communicator sounded. Planetary security headquarters for Ekhas was calling him to report that according to the department assigned to surveillance over all electronicommunications in the Naral System, examination of the information stored in the memory banks of the Terran ship's positronicon had revealed the Terrans had sent no distress call or any other messages since reemerging into the normal space-time continuum.

Egg-or did not even bother to thank his informant for the report. It was not certain enough for him. He required 100% certainty—had the *Tigris* called for help or had its crew been too surprised by the events?—and that certainty could be supplied only by examination of the memory storage units in the Terran hypercom installation.

The memory center was coupled with the hypercom just behind the microphone and the loudspeaker; beyond them were connected the encoder and the scrambler.

The 3 Ekhonide specialists did not reach what should have been an obvious conclusion: that through a simple flick of a switch the encoder and scrambler could be turned on before the hypercom's storage bank and microphone-loudspeaker systems. Nevertheless they discovered something.

It could not be perceived acoustically; and even with the help of their optical-positronic equipment they were unable to make visible the curve that is typical of a hypercom transmission. Only the Lar Detector, a device that functioned rather like a potentiometer, showed that a maximum use of energy, enduring for an improbably brief instant in time, had taken place in the recent past.

Again the Lar Detector registered the effect but the specialists looked at each other in silence. "Without importance," said the oldest at length.

"Perhaps this is the up-to-now inexplicable Echo Effect," ventured the youngest so doubtfully that Egg-Or noticed and entered into the discussion. He did not know what an Echo Effect was, at least as far as the hypercom was concerned.

The youngest of the 3 Ekhonide experts explained it briefly: "According to the theory, the Echo Effect should result when 2 hypercoms at different locations have their receivers tuned to the same wavelength. When one hypercom is transmitting, the 2d will echo the 1st and rebroadcast fragments of the transmission at full power. However, this is only theory and has never been proven."

Egg-Or was not ready to take the slightest risk. "Alright then, take this hypercom unit apart and examine every component as minutely as possible . . ."

He was interrupted. The youngest specialist claimed to have found out now why the Lar Detector had indicated a maximum use of energy. "Excuse me, sir . . .

Please take a look for yourself . . ." And then he launched into a long-winded explanation that concluded by saying that the *Tigris* had transmitted no hypercom message since emerging into normal space for the las-time.

8 hours later, Egg-Or made his report to General Sutokk, commander of the Arkonide fleet stationed on Ekhas.

Sutokk, who to Clyde Ostal had been most arrogant during the boarding operation, nodded affably to Egg-Or. "So I can without hesitation report to the Robot Regent that we are running no danger of being disturbed by Perry Rhodan if we hold onto the ship and its crew?"

Egg-Or bowed to the General and with a confident voice assured him: "General, our specialists are even now working out the data that will give us the exact galactic position of the Earth. I can't report unqualified success in that important matter yet, but in all other points I can safely say to you that your capture of the *Tigris* has not endangered us in the slightest."

"The cooperation between the Ekhonide planetary defense and the fleet of the Regent of Arkon has never been as good as it is now," Sutokk declared, then asked pressingly: "How long will it take your scientists to figure out the Earth's galactic coordinates from the data in the Terran positronicon's memory banks? Egg-Or, you know as well as I do that the Robot Regent wants that question answered as soon as possible. You remember my last hypercom conversation with the Regent, of course . . . so when can we have it, Egg-Or?"

"In 3 days at the earliest, General . . ."

"Have you gone mad? The Robot Regent would tear my commander's stripes off personally if I sent a message

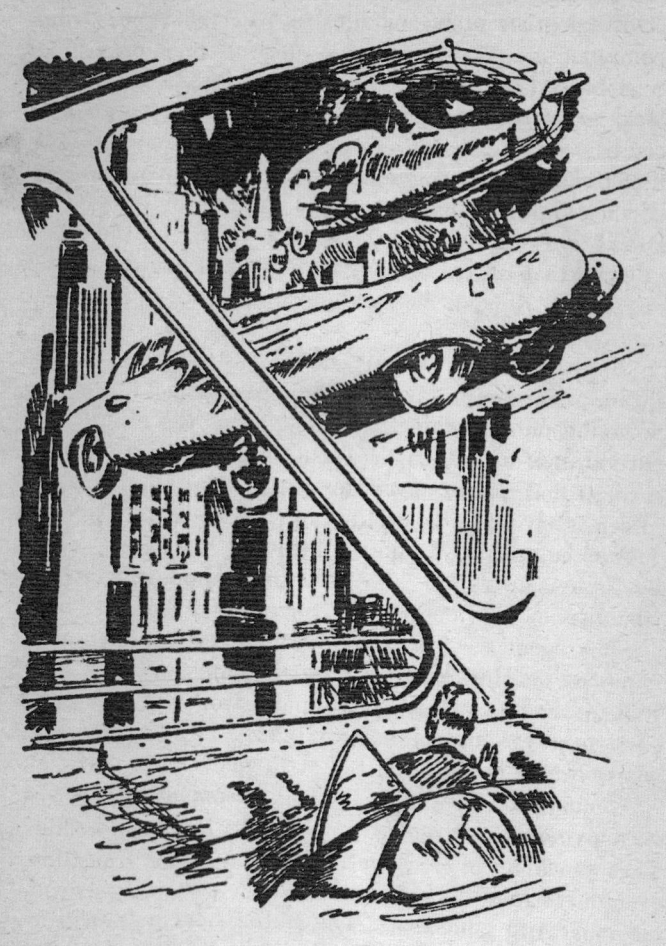

to it like that. And it wouldn't treat you any more kindly, either, *Ex*-Security Chief Egg-Or!"

Now Egg-Or demonstrated that he had a backbone. "Our scientists aren't magicians, General. A positronicomputer is a little more complicated than an adding machine. At the moment our 3 largest positronicons are busy sorting out the data contained in the Terran memory banks and calculating from it. Don't forget, General, that these calculations are extremely difficult since none of the 3 spatial coordinates nor the time constant are known to us . . ."

"What nonsense, Egg-Or!" the General interrupted. "The time constant is immutable and doesn't change . . ."

"But it becomes subject to change with every transition into hyperspace," Egg-Or retorted in a self-assured voice. "Anyway, we have learned that the *Tigris* had tried to reach the Tatlira System directly from Terra in a single spring. Isn't that already an important piece of information? But we haven't found out yet why the *Tigris* made such a crucial error in springing . . . General?" Egg-Or had suddenly noticed that Sutokk was staring pensively at him.

"Egg-Or, I just had a terrible thought. What if this misspring of the *Tigris* was nothing more than a ruse Rhodan set up to deceive the Regent? And if Rhodan is even now lurking on the edges of our system somewhere . . ."

"General," Egg-Or interrupted, smiling, "have you forgotten your new structocomp-sensor on board your ship? That piece of equipment will register any transition, even one made under the cover of one of Rhodan's structocomps. And may I inform you that our galactic surveillance operation had cracked the Terran merchant code again and that the freight run of the *Tigris* to Goszul's Planet in the Tatlira System has been known to us for days? If you like, I can supply all the relevant information for your examination."

Gen. Sutokk was still not completely reassured. Pointedly he asked the head of Ekhonide defense: "Are you absolutely certain that the *Tigris* did not deliberately misspring and that this is not a decoy operation of Rhodan's? You don't have to give me an answer now, Egg-Or. Just give the freighter captain a brainwash and if it turns out all my fears were ungrounded, I'll even be willing to call the Robot Regent and tell it that we'll need 3 days to find out the galactic coordinates of Rhodan's solar system."

Egg-Or shook his head. "No brainwashing, General. It violates our laws . . ."

"The 88 devils of the 8 stars can take those laws and—!"

"No, General, I would even refuse a direct order from the Regent on this point!"

The general smiled sarcastically at him. "As if you had any other scruples! Turn the crew of the *Tigris* over to me, Egg-Or."

"Not now, General! Not one man! Deport them, disperse them all over the Empire so that no one will ever find them again . . . alright, why not? But to make a man a mental cripple, which is always the result of a brainwash . . . No General! And that's my last word on this subject!" Egg-Or no longer had a drop of blood in his face. He felt his knees tremble but he knew that it was the only answer he could give and still be able to live with himself.

"In a few minutes I will have a very interesting little talk with the Regent," Sutokk threatened and the look in his eyes showed that he meant to carry his threat out.

At the same moment Egg-Or had switched on his pockom*. "Egg-Or here," he announced. "Message to Star Of Arkon, top priority. Not one of the incarcerated Terrans is to be . . ."

He got no farther. A stammer of words from the small but loud receiver interrupted him. "Sir . . . all 33 Terrans have broken out! The alarm just came in from the Star Of Arkon . . .!"

Egg-Or turned the communicator off and he and Sutokk stared at each other.

The mental image of each was the same: they thought of the top 5th of the towering hotel skyscraper where the prison was located. Both asked themselves how anyone could escape from that prison? Up to this day not one escape attempt had ever succeeded!

"All 33 . . .!" Egg-Or whispered.

Then he heard Sutokk's hard laughter. "It's all turning out for the best, after all," Sutokk said indolently. "Don't let your conscience bother you, Egg-Or. The chances are that at least some of these escapees will be caught by Arkonide Fleet personnel. Then I'll be able to have one or more of the Terrans brainwashed. Egg-Or, I thank you heartily for your visit to the headquarters of the Regent's fleet stationed on Ekhas. Good day . . ."

Egg-Or was anything but calm. Anger flashed in his eyes. "General," he said sharply, "this morning I insulted a Terran when we were bringing them to the prison. He did not meekly accept the insult without a word but in his reply he thanked whatever gods Terrans believe in that he was not born an Ekhonide. And General, you have just given me the proof that it *is* possible for some-

---

* Pocket communicator

one not to be proud of being an Ekhonide . . . Brain-washing, General! Are we and the Arkonide Imperium so weak and feeble that we must resort to the foulest and most contemptible means of brute force available? Isn't it enough already that the Regent thinks only in numbers and treats us like ciphers? We——"

"Egg-Or, the Regent has instructed us to find out once & for all where Rhodan's homeworld is located and I intend to carry that mission out! How I do it is something you can leave to me and the fleet. What you and your organization do is a matter that does not interest me in the least. What does interest me is whether or not Rhodan is lying in wait near our solar system."

The tension between the 2 men had ebbed somewhat.

Egg-Or declared positively: "Rhodan is *not* anywhere in the neighborhood of our solar system! The *Tigris* missprang and nothing else!"

50 ADVENTURES FROM NOW
You'll learn the
Heritage of the Lizard People

4/ PIRATICAL POSITRONICON

Perry Rhodan *was* somewhere in the neighborhood of the Naral System!

As specified in Order 22 for the *Tigris*, Maj. Clyde Ostal had half an hour at his disposal in which to make the decisive "misspring".

In Terrania, capital city of the Solar Imperium and site of the largest spaceport in the solar system, time ran inevitably towards the hour given in Order 22.

The engines of the *Lotus*, a light cruiser in the Solar Spacefleet, ran at 10% capacity. The hatches of the spacesphere were still open and all the ramps had been extended out from between the massive telescopic legs. The thundering roar emanating from the equatorial rim was a familiar sound to the men who worked at the spaceport day in & day out and hardly anyone even looked up when such a ship took off. Only the liftoff of a superbattleship of 1500 meters diameter, an incredible sight, attracted any attention. When a *Titan*-class starship blasted into the sky, that was an unforgettable experience for anyone.

But who was interested if the *Lotus* were ready for taking off? Only a few knew that Perry Rhodan had made it his flagship. Another factor that made the *Lotus* even more unique among the ships of the Terran spacefleet was known only to Perry Rhodan and a few hundred Swoons whose trustworthiness and silence was already proverbial. It had been those "Pickle-people" who had irritated Reginald Bell because he, like all other men, was simply not able to see their microscopic handiwork which they had installed in the *Lotus*.

Yet the crew of the *Lotus* was beginning to wonder about the coming mission for they had discovered that members of the secret Mutant Corps were aboard.

Tako Kakuta had not taken the normal way to his cabin: the Japanese had chosen to leave his quarters in Terrania by teleportation and materialized in Cabin 7 on C-Deck. He had returned to existence in a shimmering aura of light, carrying with him his pack of personal belongings and items necessary for the mission to come. He immediately began to unpack and stow his gear away.

His movements made the small, slender Oriental seem as harmless as a child. His boyish face only emphasized the impression and nothing about him hinted that this man was a first-class teleporter able to transport himself over almost any distance by nothing more than the strength of his will, no matter whether he could actually see his goal or merely pictured it in his mind.

Like any other mortals Fellmer Lloyd and Kitai Ishibashi had to enter the ship by way of the hatch. Shortly after these 2 mutants came on board, Perry Rhodan himself arrived.

In the control room the commander wordlessly handed Rhodan the text of a hypercom message that had just been received. It came from the *Tigris* and announced its transition with landing to follow on Goszul's Planet in the Tatlira System.

"Thank you," said Perry Rhodan and shoved the message in his pocket. He sat down in the reserve seat next to the pilot. "We can take off now," he told the ship's commander. Then he turned his head, for his 3 mutants had made their appearance and were reporting in. Once again Perry Rhodan said "Thank you" and with that his 3 special agents were dismissed.

The officers in the control room were not surprised about anything anymore. Too often they had flown similar missions and again and again experienced the almost unbelievable precision with which all preparations were made.

The light cruiser *Lotus* took off. Powerful antigravity fields raised its weight ever higher into the sky and the engines roaring at 10% capacity in the equatorial rim increased their thrust.

However, the pull of gravity inside the spacesphere remained unchanged and not even inertia exerted any perceptible influence. Precisely calculated absorbers took up the pressure before the men aboard had a chance to feel it.

The *Lotus* had gone into action.

The 2d part of a commando operation whose outcome no one could foresee began.

But Perry Rhodan did not let himself be concerned, or at least outwardly. His calm influenced everyone in the control room.

The *Lotus* reached the orbit of Pluto on schedule. A short message to the relay station on Pluto, a brief reply and at the same time clearance for the voyage into interstellar space, were the last contacts with the home solar system.

The *Lotus* approached the speed of light with ever-increasing speed and with that the moment of transition came closer.

At X minus 2 minutes, the commander of the *Lotus* looked at Rhodan. "Sir," he began, "is it true what the rumors say that the Arkonides have some new kind of sensing device that can detect hypersprings despite our structocomps?"

Rhodan smiled slightly. "The rumor is true, alright, and if you're astounded by my answer, I'm just as astounded that you've heard about this matter."

That was a clear request from Rhodan to explain the source of his knowledge. "I heard it somewhere, sir . . . and on my honor, I don't know who told me."

Perry Rhodan's gaze became stern. "I believe you," he said after a short pause, "but I think that when we get back you ought to go see Allan D. Mercant and tell him about this."

10 seconds later the *Lotus* went into transition, crossing 4535 light-years in a single spring, re-emerging into normal space about 1 light-year from the Naral System.

In the next 18 minutes nothing happened except that the *Lotus* had braked almost completely and was virtually standing still in space.

Suddenly the structure sensor showed a continuum disturbance at a distance of 1 light-year: shortly thereafter 3 further disturbances followed at the same distance and in the same direction as the first.

The intercom sounded and the Com Center reported: "Hypercom message from the *Tigris* received under encoder and scrambler. Text of the message: Ship spotted!"

Perry Rhodan turned his head to the commander. "Order B/3!"

Almost in the same breath the commander called out: "Carry out prepared transition!"

The short transition brought the *Tigris* some 20 light-days closer to the Naral System. When all the other crew members were still shaking off the effects of the transition shock, Perry Rhodan sat almost unaffected in the reserve seat and looked almost impassively in the direction of the structure-sensor. Inwardly he fought to hold down his excitement.

He was the only one aboard who knew what the next few minutes meant for the Solar Imperium.

When the 5th minute went by, Rhodan told himself that he had spent long enough waiting for something that was not going to happen.

The inhuman, grinding tension fell away from him. He felt like he was coming back to life and the 2 officers at the structure-sensor discreetly wiped the sweat from their foreheads.

"The *Lotus* hasn't been spotted . . .!"

And Perry Rhodan smiled, amused at being stared at from all sides. Some faces were questioning, others were completely at a loss.

He was only human and he needed to unwind from tension, to relax like any other human. The questioning faces and the uncomprehending expressions were *his* relaxation, and that relaxation gave him fresh strength to replace that lost in answering the question "Is there a means to render the Arkonide sensing device inoperable?"

And there was a means!

It had just passed its final test: the *Lotus* had not been detected!

The new device, the Frequency Damper, a counter-development to the Arkonide Compensator Detector, was the product of the Swoon technicians who earlier had voluntarily left their world to go with Perry Rhodan and begin a new life on Terra.

He had them and their skills to thank for the damper that neutralized the vibrations given off by the structo-comp and thus effectively put a crimp in Arkonide plans to learn the position of the Earth with the help of their Compensator Detector.

"Yes, gentlemen," said Perry Rhodan, laughing heartily, "it is indeed a miracle that this ship was *not* detected after its 2 transitions. The *Tigris* was spotted in spite of its structocomp. Don't look at me with such disbelief. Perhaps Arkon does have a device that can detect and measure each and every hyperspring . . . but the *Lotus* is now out of its range, so to speak. This is the only Terran spaceship equipped with a frequency damper but I hope that in a month all Terran spacers will have such equipment. That's assuming, of course, that the Swoons can build so many auxiliary devices for the structocomps in so short a time."

"The pickle people?!" exclaimed the commander, using the expression that had been applied to the little technicians the firstime man and Swoon had encountered one another.

"That's correct," said Perry Rhodan and his eyes were radiant with joy. "This swift development is something we owe entirely to our little friends."

Then a call from the Com Center brought Perry Rhodan back to cold reality.

"Sir!" exclaimed the Com Officer, gasping out his alarming news. "At this time an Arkonide ship is transmitting over hypercom on the Robot Brain's frequency!"

"Are they using a scrambler and encoder system?" Rhodan demanded.

"Yes sir," the Com Officer answered. "We know how to unscramble the message and we can slow it down from its speeded-up version—which is how they're transmitting it—but the code is unknown to us!"

After considering for a moment, Rhodan ordered:

"Feed the coded text to the positronicon and see what it can make of it!"

"They're still transmitting on the Regent frequency but we're giving the text we have already to the positronicon now, sir!"

Then, after 14 minutes, the hypercom exchange between an Arkonide ship and the Robot Regent was over. The large positronicon aboard the *Lotus* continued its attempt to find the key to the code but after 20 minutes the otherwise all but omnicompetent machine gave up. A small strip of tape fell into the receptacle—a request for more additional information.

"There's no point in it now," Rhodan decided and left the reserve seat. Bidding his men farewell, he went to the hatchway that separated the Com Center and the control room from the rest of the spacer and walked across the broad A-Deck to his cabin.

The 14-minute exchange between an Arkonide spacer and the Robot Brain had given Rhodan more to think about than he had let on in the control room. Once more his suspicion, that the giant positronicon on Arkon 3, absolute ruler of the Great Imperium, had no scruples in its soulless logic against treason and deception, had almost become a certainty.

Rhodan thought of the mysterious Druufs, those powerful beings from the 2d time-plane, who continually penetrated this dimension during overlappings of the 2 universes to abduct millions and billions of living creatures.

The Robot Brain had allied itself with him to combat this uncanny enemy and Rhodan had been named Commander-In-Chief over Arkon's gigantic spacefleet. However, he could exercise his authority only for the fight against the Druufs and not for matters involving other interests.

Perry Rhodan smiled grimly. Once again he had been reminded that the friendship alliance between him and Arkon was nothing more than a temporary arrangement made necessary by a common enemy. Meanwhile, the mammoth positronicon was attempting unceasingly by any means no matter how foul to learn Earth's galactic position. Evidently it did not even hesitate to act like a pirate and capture a Terran ship that had erred in making a transition just to loot its memory banks for the Sol System's coordinates.

Shortly before the *Tigris* had taken off, Rhodan had given Maj. Clyde Ostal the order to contact the Terran trading outpost on Goszul's Planet, 3 hours after making the transition into the Naral System.

Now Perry Rhodan had to let those 3 hours tick by. When all but 20 minutes of the time period had elapsed, Rhodan called the control room over the intercom and told the commander: "Prepare for Order B/7, Commander. Carry out only when I specifically tell you to!"

Order B/7 concerned a new transition which would bring the *Lotus* into the welter of stars in the center of the Milky Way.

Rhodan's choice of a new destination had been carefully thought out: it was far from all traveled routes and, moreover, it would be avoided by even the bravest Arkonides like the plague.

The region was 100 light-years in diameter, dominated by 4 monstrous, invisible and energy-rich radio stars which possessed magnetic fields of unimaginable intensity as well—making navigation in this sector almost impossible and paralyzing hypercom traffic.

Perry Rhodan knew precisely which of the rumors

about this place were correct and which were only legends old spacemen might swap. The firstime he had been in the area had been with the *Titan* and on the other 2 occasions he had taken the *Drusus*. Ce had encountered improbable conditions that could be explained only by the magnetic fields of the radio stars which reached deep into space. However, this place in the universe lost all its terrors for someone who learned how to conduct himself there.

Rhodan's well-developed sense of time led him to glance at the chronometer. The 3d hour was just coming to an end.

Order B/7 was to be carried out!

The universe seemed to explode in front of the *Lotus* and the ship disappeared, rematerializing in the same instant in the center of the galaxy.

5 minutes later Rhodan was in the Com Center. "Call the *Mab* 1, codeword Arkon. You'll find the hypercom frequency listed in the printed wavelength guide. Bring the reply to my cabin."

Then he instructed that the mutants be sent to him. Even Tako Kakuta, the teleporter, arrived by the normal way.

Fellmer Lloyd, the muscular and dark-haired locater and telepath who could not only perceive brainwaves and analyze them but also sense other people's moods and feel oncoming danger far in advance, had a clumsy, ponderous look to him.

Quite the opposite was Kitai Ishibashi—who had been a doctor and psychologist before joining Rhodan's mutant corps. He was tall, slender and perhaps fit the mold of an intellectual. As a suggestor he was all but an indispensable member of the corps.

"Just a few minutes ago," said Rhodan, "I informed the

galactic trader Mabdan that I'm waiting for him at the agreed-upon place. We will board his ship, the *Mab* 1, fly with it to the Naral System and land at the Ent-Than spaceport." Rhodan smiled a little as he looked at the suggestor and continued, "Ishibashi, you had better go talk to the commander of the *Lotus* right now and let him know how you plan to work. I'd rather not run any unnecessary risks on this mission, especially not with the *Lotus* and its new frequency damper involved. You're the only one who can contact the ship and its commander from Ekhas—even though in only a suggestive fashion. Fill him in so that no one has to be unpleasantly surprised.

"The *Mab* 1 will be alongside in an hour at most. We'll cross over in Springer spacesuits and we won't be taking any Terran equipment with us. Please check even your clothing over carefully with that in mind.

"The Ekhonides are Arkonides! If we never forget that, we'll never underestimate them."

Rhodan looked at his men thoughtfully. A vague disquiet was bothering him and several times his thoughts centered around Mabdan. That galactic trader was an agent for Earth like many others of his race.

Mabdan belonged to the agents who had worked longest for Rhodan but under one thin pretense or another he had managed to avoid the last 3 thought-probes by Terran telepaths. It was a matter of bad luck that Allan D. Mercant had to call on Mabdan, no one else being available, for the flight to Ekhas.

The press of time which had affected the whole mission from the beginning had simply not allowed the Terrans to find a more trustworthy Springer than Mabdan.

Rhodan spoke to Fellmer Lloyd. "Check the Springer

Mabdan's mind as soon as we step aboard. I have my suspicions, Lloyd!"

Soon the *Mab* 1 was alongside the *Lotus;* Perry Rhodan and his 3 mutants floated in Springer spacesuits over to it. The make-up artist aboard the *Lotus* had produced his masterpiece: even Perry Rhodan would not have recognized himself in the mirror and he entered the hatch of the *Mab* 1 as Alf Renning.

A young Springer received them with a broad smile. His Interkosmo sprinkled liberally with slang, he invited them to come with him to his "Master".

Unsuspecting, the 4 Terrans entered the expansive cabin. Then Fellmer Lloyd telepathed his chief, *This isn't him! It's Mabdan 3!*

The number following the clan name indicated the rank of the Springer bearing it, and numbers up to 50 were not uncommon.

Mabdan 3 came towards them with a friendly expression on his face. He radiated calmness and trust. His invitation to sit down seemed hearty enough and Fellmer Lloyd could find nothing dangerous in the Springer's thoughts after examining them with the greatest concentration.

While the discussion turned around risk, danger and payments, and Perry Rhodan silently pushed a large sum of money to the Springer, Fellmer Lloyd perceived another set of thought emanations. They came from somewhere aboard the ship but they could not be clearly made out or identified.

Lloyd glanced innocently over at Kitai Ishibashi, who was just then relating some amusing space anecdote. It brought Mabdan 3 to laughing but suddenly the Springer's laugh died away.

"What did you just say, Terran?" he demanded quickly and his face grew pale.

The tall, thin Oriental smiled his unfathomable smile. "Mabdan 3, I said . . ."

And then, grinning, the Springer had an impulse beamer in his hand.

Fellmer Lloyd desperately wondered why he hadn't sensed this coming while sitting directly across from the compactly built Springer with the carefully trimmed beard.

Lloyd felt no fear. The galactic trader had already passed up his only chance to kill anyone with the beamer by waiting too long. Kitai Ishibashi was already "treating" him. Ever more strongly the slender Oriental forced Mabdan 3 under his will. He was confident of his success and overlooked the fact he had already ordered the Springer twice to lay the impulse beamer on the table.

But Mabdan 3 had no such intentions.

The malicious grin was still spread across his face. He opened his mouth to speak. Then an inexplicable flickering in the air frightened him and his fright became panic when the shortest of the Terrans materialized next to him. The Terran's hand shot out and knocked the beamer out of the Springer's grasp and then Mabdan 3 found himself at the mercy of a thermobeamer trained directly at him.

Tako Kakuta had reversed the situation with 1 short teleportation spring.

Fellmer Lloyd, who looked so clumsy, acted astonishingly fast. He swiftly disarmed the completely confused Mabdan 3 and threw a psychobeamer of the latest Arkonide model and a paralyser on the table.

In his panic Mabdan 3 did not notice Alf Renning giving his slim companion a brief but sharp glance. Concentrating with unusual strength, Ishibashi attempted to force his will on the Springer but to no avail. It was almost as if Mabdan 3 did not exist at all, for all the effect Ishibashi's efforts had.

"I'm not getting anywhere with him either," said Fellmer Lloyd in English. "I can't get a clear picture of his brainwave pattern and his emotional patterns have completely changed—I can't get a clear picture of them, either."

These words were directed to Perry Rhodan, who had not moved since the appearance of the impulse beamer. Only his eyes were moving, glancing from here to there. Now he fixed his gaze on the Springer once more. The galactic trader's eyes presented a riddle for him.

However, Rhodan did not have a chance to solve the riddle.

"There's danger coming from the deck!" Fellmer Lloyd warned, stepping behind Mabdan 3 and forcing the Springer's hands behind his back.

A moment later the commandeered weapons had been divided among the Terrans. Only Lloyd had not taken part: he had to concern himself with Mabdan 3 and continue his attempt to probe the Springer's thoughts.

"The danger is coming closer!" he signaled Rhodan and his comrades. "2 men. They're coming for us!"

Fellmer Lloyd was not able to penetrate the Springer's thoughts. Something was protecting them from his probing mind.

The door opened slowly and the faces of the 2 entering Springers went white when they saw the 3 weapons aimed at them. Without waiting to be told they dropped their psychobeamers.

"Ishibashi . . ." Rhodan only pronounced his name as he ordered with an imperious movement of his head for the Springers to enter the cabin completely. The suggestor was already active at this time and Mabdan 3 thought he was dreaming when he saw the inexplicable change in attitude of his 2 shipmates who suddenly smiled at the Terrans, spoke in a friendly manner to them and without being asked sat down and made themselves comfortable.

"Mabdan 3 has been blocked, men!" Rhodan said without further commentary.

Katai Ishibashi, the most intelligent of the 3 mutants, understood at once what Rhodan meant.

That part of Operation Naral System involving the active participation of Springer Agent Mabdan 1 had been betrayed. And in that case the Robot Brain's defensive section must have reacted instantly.

In the place of Mabdan 1, Terran agent, and ignoring the order of Springer ranking, Mabdan 3 had been prepared.

A hypnotic block lay upon the Springer's mind and Kitai Ishibashi was unable to remove it. The Oriental's suggestive power was psychic in origin whereas Mabdan 3's blockade was the work of an Arkonide hypno-machine which, in its soulless fulfillment of its assigned task, did not hesitate to mercilessly distort the Springer's brainwave pattern.

Mabdan 3 did not understand that he would soon go insane unless Rhodan's mutants soon found a way to remove the artificial hypnoblock.

Fellmer Lloyd, still trying to understand what Rhodan had said, was startled. Once again he had sensed a strange brainwave pattern, and again only vaguely.

He began to search.

There it was again. In a sort of trance, he described to Tako Kakuta the layout of the cabin from which the strange brainwave pattern came.

Perry Rhodan had no objection to Kakuta's teleportational spring.

The 2 Springers were still under the power of Ishibashi and he gave them the order not to look at what happened in the cabin.

The slender teleporter disappeared in a flickering light in the air from Mabdan 3's cabin. Mabdan 3 himself thought of ghosts and devils while his 2 men sat harmlessly in a corner and chatted, taking no apparent notice of the odd goings on.

Now Lloyd entered into telepathicontact with Kakuta.

Kakuta had materialized in a small cabin at the end of the spacious deck and found an unconscious man who had a surprising resemblance to Mabdan 3.

Fellmer Lloyd did not have to say anything. Perry Rhodan had tuned in himself. By way of their telepathicontact with Kakuta they witnessed along with him what was to be found in the small cabin, for under these favorable circumstances—Rhodan stood right next to Lloyd—Rhodan was able to receive Lloyd's thoughts.

I know about this poison, don't I? The Aras brew it, right? It's a time-stopping drug that reduces all bodily functions down to an absolute minimum. 4 breaths in 1 minute . . .

Then the telepathicontact between Fellmer Lloyd and Tako Kakuta broke off temporarily.

"Kakuta is to come back here and spring to the Com Center with Ishibashi, Lloyd!" Rhodan ordered in English.

In the next instant the air behind Mabdan 3 flickered and the small, slender teleporter had returned.

Kitai Ishibashi stood next to Kakuta and waited for Rhodan's final instructions. "Transmit an emergency call to the *Lotus* using the equipment in the *Mab* 1's Com Center. The *Lotus* is to get as fast as possible, Alarm Level #1! They are to send over a commando team 10 men strong with a dozen battle robots!"

While Rhodan was still speaking, Kitai Ishibashi rested his hand on the slender teleporter's shoulder. He neither felt nor saw anything as the small man dematerialized with him and rematerialized at the same moment in the Com Center of the cylinder ship.

Before the 3 Springers on duty in the Com Center could turn around upon hearing the slight noise of the 2 Terrans materializing, Ishibashi employed his strongest suggestive powers on them.

"Let me sit down here for a minute, old friend!" Kakuta told the Springer at the hypercom transmitter.

Without a word, the young galactic trader stood up and gave his seat to the Terran. His 2 comrades saw nothing peculiar about it—and as Tako Kakuta sent his message, they sat off by themselves, deep in conversation and laughing over some joke.

Shortly thereafter, the Springers were back on communications duty. They had no memory of any visitors to the Com Center. However, instead of leaving gaping holes in their minds, Ishibashi had filled the gaps with his suggestive power, and his implanted memories had become reality for the Springers.

Mabdan 3, still sitting defenseless in his seat, no longer followed the comings & goings behind his back. Whatever the Terrans were discussing in their own language remained a mystery to him.

Kakuta teleported into the cabin of the unconscious

Springer for the 2d time. He was to attempt to find out more about the man.

"Where is Mabdan 2?" Rhodan demanded sharply of Mabdan 3. "We've found the clan chieftain unconscious in a small cabin . . . your clan is going to wonder in a few days why you are playing the role of your patriarch. And then, my friend, I think you'll have some very unpleasant minutes ahead of you. Now, where is Mabdan 2, Springer?"

Perry Rhodan's warning made no impression on the defenseless man. Kitai Ishibashi told his chief as much. "It's not getting through to him at all, sir. I have—"

"Ah, Perry Rhodan!" exclaimed the Springer, his face distorted.

Kitai Ishibashi had made the inexcusable error of addressing Rhodan with the word "sir". He telepathed Kakuta, hoping that setting the teleporter into immediate action would at least halfway make up for his mistake. *Kakuta, spring at once into the Com Center! Look to see if there isn't a 2d hypercom unit that's transmitting the conversation here in the cabin. Hurry, Kakuta!*

In that moment, Perry Rhodan, the Administrator of the Solar Imperium, became conscious when Mabdan 3 cried out his name that the giant positronic brain on Arkon 3 knew only *one* goal: learning Earth's galactic position at any cost and by any means, and then eliminating the threat of Perry Rhodan and his Solar Imperium by making it into an Arkonide colony.

The Robot Regent had assembled all data that could possibly lead to the identification of Perry Rhodan and the English title "sir" was one such identifying datum!

Rhodan's thoughts raced farther. It surprised him that Mabdan 3 had betrayed his discovery in such a stupid manner. At that point Fellmer Lloyd interrupted his consideration of the problem. "Sir, Mabdan 3's brainwave pattern . . . I've never seen anything like it, not even with insane persons . . ."

And then Fellmer Lloyd was interrupted, as well.

Kakuta appeared in a shimmering of air. His face was bruised and he was bleeding from the left temple. But he paid no attention to that. His report was more important to him now than his own life. "Every word, everything that was said here, was transmitted by a 2d hypercom, transmitted on the Robot Regent frequency . . . up to 2 minutes ago. But not any more . . ." And the slender Oriental showed his thermobeamer to Perry Rhodan with an apologetic gesture. "I used this on the hypercom. But the damage has been done, there's nothing we can do about it now. I'm just surprised that Arkon hasn't sent a few dozen superbattleships out here already with a friendly invitation for us to come aboard . . ."

"I'm not at all surprised," said Perry Rhodan and there seemed to be laughter in his gray eyes. After all, he knew this part of the universe and its 4 invisible radio stars.

100 ADVENTURES FROM NOW
You'll watch as
Four Powers Fight

5/ THE STARHELL

The Ekhonide prison administration for the Star of Arkon had its own opinions about the matter of hygiene and so far had had good results, especially with newly arrived prisoners from outer space.

Processing the entry of each new prisoner was quickly accomplished with the help of positronic equipment but despite first class Ara methods disinfection took up a relatively large amount of time.

Maj. Clyde Ostal and his men went from one surprise to the next without any time to recover from the first.

Just now they were being sent to the 7th department; no one felt very much at ease about it. They were taken up by antigrav lift for a "Virospectroscopic Examination".

The Virospectroscopic Department was on the top floor of the huge skyscraper and took up a good third of that level.

6 Ekhonides armed with shock weapons brought them to the entrance. As in the 6 preceding medical departments, the guards remained outside while the Terrans went in.

Maj. Clyde Ostal waved him away hastily when Lt. S. Seeger wanted to talk to him. The Terrans were lined up 2 by 2 and Ostal was in front of Seeger. Then the entranceway was sealed off by a powerful energy screen. Maj. Ostal did not notice: a small sidedoor through which Ekhonide medics were coming & going attracted his attention.

Now he saw that the sidedoor was open again and that it was staying open longer than usual. An older Ekhonide stood in the doorway, calling something up above.

Up above . . . that was a moving walkway leading sharply upwards. Beyond it Ostal could see a narrow stripe of the blue, cloudless sky of Ekhas.

"Here comes Hasting," Ostal heard Lt. Seeger say.

At that moment the major understood that Hasting, who had broken his arm by falling against the energy barrier at the entrance to the prison, had been treated. He whispered sharply to Lt. Seeger: "Bring Hasting over here!"

They were still waiting in the large, long-stretching anteroom of the Virospectroscopic department. The walls and ceiling were coated with a white plastic substance and the room was lighted indirectly from all sides. The Ekhonides passing through the room on business stared at the Terrans as though they were strange animals.

Maj. Clyde Ostal glanced at the small sidedoor. It was still open and the old Ekhonide was still standing in the doorway. The tiny bit of cloudless blue Ekhonide sky was still visible, too.

And wasn't that the typical noise of an Arkonide air-taxi starting up, coming through the open doorway?

Maj. Ostal felt a hand on his shoulder. It was Seeger, who was saying to him in a muted voice: "Hasting is here with us but . . ."

The small side door closed. The old Ekhonide crossed the large anteroom and disappeared behind a transparent door, through which was visible a room with a large number of flashing devices inside.

"Men!" Clyde Ostal's sharp but muted call drew their attention. "Keep it down but go on as before . . . keep on talking but listen to me!

"Over on the left, that small sidedoor leads up to a flight deck on the roof! When I say the word *Tigris*, make sure that no Ekhonide has a chance to cry out. It won't hurt to be safe and it won't cost more than 3 seconds time. Then leave by the sidedoor. A rollband leads up to the roof. What we'll run into up there, I don't know . . ." Here the major saw that there were only 3 Ekhonides with them in the spacious anteroom.

He gave the signal. *"Tigris."* Even though all the Terrans were stark naked, they were dangerous and ready for anything. It was not for nothing that the Chief of Solar Defense, Allan D. Mercant, had a reputation of always being on the lookout for new methods of teaching his men better ways in which to cope with the dangers they met almost daily while in service for the Solar Imperium.

3 unsuspecting Ekhonides, doctors in service for the Justice Department of Ekhas, suddenly saw naked Terrans in front of them—then they saw only shadowy fists flying at them and after that they saw and heard nothing more. They felt nothing more for they lay unconscious on the floor while 33 pairs of naked feet hurried towards the small sidedoor. Maj. Clyde Ostal had opened it by laying his left hand on the rosette in the middle of the door.

Once on the rollband which carried him swiftly upwards to the flightdeck on the roof, he turned around. In perfect order, as though on the way to an exercise field, his men left the large anteroom.

They came out one after another and stepped onto the rollband, which appeared perfectly capable of bearing the steadily increasing weight.

Clyde Ostal reached the roof in 4 seconds. The brilliant light of the yellowish shining sun of Naral blinded him. Squinting against the glare, he glanced from right to left. He had expected heavily armed guards waiting at the end of the rollband and he was astounded that there were none.

"Everybody's out, Major!" someone called from below.

In 4 seconds the last of his men would have reached the roof. He stepped aside to give them room.

From the left came a shout!

On the left travelers were leaving an airtaxi that had just brought them here from the spaceport.

But on the right, not 20 paces away, stood an identical airtaxi with an extended but motionless rollband.

"Let them yell . . . !" Maj. Clyde Ostal called over his shoulder to his men, who were coming up to the roof 2 by 2 on the rollband. "Head for the taxi there on the right!"

3 seconds had gone by. 8 of his men were still on the rollband. With 24 of his men behind him, he ran for the taxi. "Seeger!" he exclaimed and got a reply from the right instantly. "Seeger, come with me—the others go in the passenger cabin!"

Clyde Ostal made a running leap towards the airtaxi, grabbed the handholds projecting from the sides and pulled himself up into the pilot's chamber.

Lt. Seeger followed immediately after, closing the door quickly behind him. "The last ones are coming, Major . . . but, good heavens! Those Ekhonides on the roof will *never* forget *us!*"

From the passenger cabin came the shout: "All here, Major!" At the same time the broad cabin door closed with a hollow thud and the rollband was drawn in up under the taxi's hull.

Ostal, who had immediately turned on the engines, did not worry about whether he could take off so soon with such a heavy load or not.

The engines roared. The airtaxi lifted from the flight-deck and climbed 20 meters straight up. Then Clyde Ostal turned the airtaxi in the direction of that dark stripe in the north far beyond Ent-Than which he had recognized as a forest area during the landing maneuvers of the *Tigris*. He gave the airtaxi full thrust.

Seeger sat in front of the radio. In spite of the roaring engines, Ostal listened too. As yet none of the wavelengths Seeger had tuned to carried any word of their escape.

How could they know that at that moment the doctors in the Virospectroscoptic Dept. assumed the Terrans were being tested in G8, while their colleagues in G8 thought they were still being examined by the Viroanalyzers?

No one had yet noticed the 3 senseless doctors lying together in a corner of the anteroom, covered with their own soft, green doctors' jackets.

The airtaxi went faster & faster. The vast sea of houses of Ent-Than slid past them below and soon the suburban settlements appeared in front of them.

Maj. Clyde Ostal's sharply profiled face looked to the distant forest edge approaching at an impossibly slow speed. He was still not quite convinced of the success of his desperate undertaking. The sensation they had unwillingly caused by their unclad appearance on the flight-deck of Ent-Than's largest hotel must certainly have its consequences.

"Nothing on the radio about us yet," remarked Seeger, grinning like a boy who has just pulled off an improbable prank with unexpectedly great success. "Major, I wonder if the hotel guests are unaware that the upper 5th of the Star of Arkon is a prison and took us for some odd race of savages on our way to our home planet?"

"Oh, cut the kidding!" Ostal told him. "You'd do better to keep your ear glued to that radio and keep watch over all channels! Is there another ship following us yet?"

The major could not know that the lieutenant's conjecture matched the truth perfectly. In that moment the administration of the hotel was under fire with complaints from all sides. Outraged tourists and guests of the Star Of Arkon, Ent-Than's most exclusive hotel, were demanding to know why quarters had been given to naked savages and why they had been allowed to take off in full view from a public flight deck.

The administration along with its robots was completely at a loss. Their statements that they knew nothing of any of this and certainly had nothing to do with those mysterious events were not believed. But no one connected the happenings with the prison in the building's upper 5th and so the authorities were not immediately notified. The prison had been located there for 208 years and in all that time not 1 prisoner had ever succeeded in escaping.

"Still nothing?" Ostal asked for the 8th time.

"No, Major!" Lt. Seeger could not remember ever being so pleased about answering a question.

The forest edge shot towards them and then it was suddenly behind them. The sea of trees beneath the airtaxi grew thicker & thicker. Now a small clearing appeared. The roaring of the overheated engines suddenly stopped. The braking equipment screeched loudly but it was enough to slow the airtaxi's fall.

It landed as gently as a feather.

The rollband slid rattling out from its slot under the rear of the airtaxi. Hissing, the automatic equipment opened the broad cabin door. 31 Terrans hastily left the airtaxi and sought cover under the first trees at the clearing's edge. Even Lt. Seeger sprang out. Maj. Clyde Ostal still had something to do: he had to somehow dispose of the airtaxi whose presence would otherwise betray the Terrans' location.

It was a daring maneuver but the major did not hesitate for even a second.

The engines began to roar again, though muted. Ostal's right hand lay on the switch that would supply full power to the machinery. Calmly but not slowly he checked over the robot-steering one more time. Set on an easterly course, the airtaxi would suddenly fall and crash from an altitude of 3000 meters after an 8 minute flight—assuming that no Ekhonide policeship had discovered by that time the airtaxi carried neither pilot nor passengers and captured it.

"Ok . . ." said Ostal to himself. He half stood up, turned to the open doorway of the pilot's cabin and then with his right hand threw the power supply switch.

Then Maj. Clyde Ostal jumped the 2 meters to the ground. Above him the mistreated engines roared in protest, shaking the airtaxi down to its last nuts & bolts.

Soft grass absorbed Ostal's fall. A shadow from above slid past him, slipped just above the tops of the first trees and then, still in the range of vision, turned to the east and climbed at a 15° angle into the sky.

A minute later the clearing was as still as it had been before the landing of the airtaxi. The roaring of the engines could no longer be heard but then a voice called out: "I'm curious to see how all this turns out!"

Maj. Ostal replied severely to the speaker: "Sgt. Brack, I can understand that this affair would have you wondering—but this is neither the time nor the place to discuss it! We won't be able to accomplish anything by just talking."

Egg-Or, head of the planetary defense for Ekhas, felt rather the same way. After a lightning trip from the headquarters of the Arkonide fleet back to his own offices, he was being briefed on the new developments in the case.

More than that, he was also reprimanding his chief of police. "Do-Man, have you notified all the clothing stores that they might be broken into tonight? . . . No? May I be so bold as to inquire when you're going to do so? This concerns all stores within a radius of 500 drans (1 dran = 1.47 kilometers). While you're at it, warn all the weapons merchants and the food vendors and anyone else it may occur to you to notify. That's all, Do-Man!"

Dragging his steps, Do-Man left the gathering. His 6 colleagues, who were not allowed to go yet, envied him. He had the worst behind him; for them it was yet to come.

But Egg-Or was a man who could do more than just upbraid his staff. Hardly had the door dropped down behind Do-Man than Egg-Or's face relaxed and he made himself more comfortable in his seat.

"We have 33 Terrans to capture again, men," he said. "We've been broadcasting their faces over the television channels for the last hour without stopping. If they weren't *Terrans*, they'd be no problem at all to apprehend. Yes, I—" Without warning the vidscreen in front of Egg-Or lit, showing the excited face of Exwin, chief of traffic control at the Ent-Than spaceport.

"Yes?" asked Egg-Or tersely, sitting up straight. He knew that a surprise was in the offing, only he could not say whether it was going to be a pleasant or an unpleasant one.

"Egg-Or, just an hour ago the *Mab* 1, first ship of the Springer clan Mabdan, landed here. Our check of its papers and cargo—a cargo being shipped to Ent-Than and so labelled—disclosed no discrepencies but a chance visit to the Com Center gleaned the knowledge that the *Mab* 1 had a second hypercom unit aboard, destroyed during the flight to Ekhas.

"Egg-Or, I wouldn't have called you had the investigation of our officials relative to the 2d hypercom and its destruction turned up a satisfactory explanation. But no member of the Springer crew could explain the purpose of the 2d unit or why it was destroyed.

"Thereupon the *Mab* 1 was put under close watch. We learned thereby that at least 4 persons more, if not 6, were on board than were carried in the crew lists. Further, Mabdan 1 was missing. The crew could give no information about the present whereabouts of the Springer patriarch and knew nothing of the presence of extra persons aboard the ship. They were all certain, however, that at the beginning of the voyage to the Naral System, Mabdan 1 had been aboard.

"Accordingly I put the *Mab* 1 under quarantine. The Springer ship is being searched again at this time and I've brought in 4 specialists to give the positronicon aboard the *Mab* 1 a thorough examination."

The longer Exwin spoke, the greater grew Egg-Or's excitement. More out of instinct than reason he saw connections between the captured *Tigris* and the just landed *Mab* 1.

"Thank you for this information, Exwin," said Egg-Or with a slightly hoarse voice. "Interrogate all the Springers intensively and separately. Put 3 or 4 men on the investigation of the ship's positronicon. Have you contacted the *Mab* 1's port of origin yet?"

"No," came Exwin's answer from the spaceport.

"Then do so immediately. Call me when you've learned anything new, no matter what time of day or night it is!"

Egg-Or switched off. He glanced almost absentmindedly at his staff. They didn't dare speak to him. Each man knew that often in the past their chief had solved problems sitting at his desk, which the entire alerted defense ministry had not been able to handle.

Egg-Or was one of those lucky individuals whose reason and intuition were equally developed. He was one of the few who often followed his hunches and set his reasoning aside.

"Now . . ." he said, sounding like someone who had just awakened from a light sleep with a start. "You know yourselves what has to be done. Set in motion every means at your disposal so that we can have those 33 Terrans back in our hands by tomorrow. If I'm not here in headquarters, I'll leave a message in any case telling where I am."

The staff left the chief somewhat confused. They had thought the meeting would proceed not a little differently and they could not shake off the feeling that the abrupt end of the conference had something to do with Exwin's call from the spaceport.

They were right. Egg-Or flew to the spaceport and entered the planetary defense department offices just as a hypercom exchange with Soral, 4.7 light-years away, was ending.

Exwin, an unusually tall Ekhonide, gave the impression to the entering Egg-Or that he was on the verge of a breakdown. He was alone with Egg-Or in the room. With an exhausted motion he switched off the microphone. "Egg-Or, did you hear who I was talking to?"

"Of course—with Soral. Did the *Mab* 1 come from that planet?"

"Yes, Egg-Or," Exwin replied, nodding, and trying to regain his composure. However, the beads of sweat he wiped from his forehead testified to a considerable shock. "But it took off from Soral for Ekhas with a gravely ill Mabdan 1 on board; and because a cylinder spacer has to have a capable captain, Mabdan 3 was put in his place although the clan was neither asked nor advised about the move. Egg-Or, now I'm asking *you* a question: where are Mabdan 1 and 3? Why is it that no Springer knew if one or the other was on board?"

"Have the galactic traders been asked how many transitions it took them to make the trip to Ekhas?"

"Yes. They all said 5, and the ship's positronicon confirms it . . ."

The loudspeaker interrupted with a question. "May Sassas see you, sir?"

Exwin spoke into the microphone. "Send Sassas in!" And to Egg-Or he said: "Sassas was one of those investigating the *Mab* 1's positronicon."

An old and bent Ekhonide entered. His face promised nothing good and neither did the sheaf of papers he held in his hand.

"Take a seat," Exwin told him. His voice sounded impatient.

The specialist sat down and handed the papers to Exwin. "Here," he said, greatly excited and pointing to the confusion of coordinates and figures covering the 8 sheets. Seen as a whole, the diagrams made an impressive flight curve. "Here is where the *Mab* 1 reentered our universe after the 4th spring. Point of entry: Restricted Zone 0674 B-00001 . . ."

"00001?" exclaimed Egg-Or in surprise while Exwin

tried to understand it. "00001, Sassas, isn't that . . . ?"

"Yes, it definitely is the Starhell! And as Starhell it's listed in the catalog of restricted areas under the number 0674 B-00001."

"Sassas, you must be mistaken," Egg-Or said firmly.

"I can make mistakes but a positronicon never does. I obtained these coordinates from the *Mab* 1's positronicon. But not only did the Springer ship search out the area of the 4 hellstars in the middle of the Milky Way for transition but it also cruised here & there in that region for over 3 hours, seemingly with no destination in mind at all, until it received a hypercom message consisting of just 1 word: 'Arkon' . . ."

"Just a moment," Egg-Or broke in, looking at Exwin and Sassas in surprise. "What does the star catalog say about the Starhell area? Doesn't it say that hypercommunication is impossible there and that the same goes for any astronavigation? Something isn't right, Sassas!"

"I'm only telling you what we found in the positronicon," said Sassas obstinately. "But isn't it noteworthy that the *Mab* 1 reached our system from the starhell in one transition . . . and as I heard, thanks to our interrogators, even without a captain!"

Egg-Or turned to Exwin. "Call Soral again. This change of command in the *Mab* 1 seems mysterious to me in a way. Every Arkonide administration is reluctant to even attempt to meddle with the customs of the Galactic Traders but has the port authority on Soral gone so far as to step in directly and interfere with the all but holy order of Springer rank? I can believe all the rest but *that* I won't! Quick, Exwin, call Soral, but don't ask for the spaceport—get the Arkonide administration."

But a hypercommunication was not yet in the cards. Gen. Sutokk called from his headquarters. His face, which had not struck Maj. Clyde Ostal as a particularly delightful one on the *Tigris* vidscreen, now gave the Ekhonide Egg-Or a somewhat unpleasant feeling as well.

"Ah, so your office has informed me correctly for once, Egg-Or," said the general mockingly when Egg-Or's face appeared on the headquarters vidscreen. "I'm calling because I've heard some odd things concerning a Springer ship. Has it ever occured to you that this merchant clan could be in league with Perry Rhodan? Leave the Springer crew to me for a few hours and my fleet officers will be able to give you the most eloquent confessions without any contradictions! Then we'll know, both of us, the whereabouts of these 4 or 6 persons who secretly came to Ekhas aboard the *Mab* 1!"

"Brainlashing, General?" asked Egg-Or sharply.

"Naturally . . ."

"Good," said Egg-Or. "I still have some business to finish, important business. When I'm done with that I'll call and tell you my decision."

"I'll be waiting for your call, Egg-Or!" With that the General switched off and his face disappeared from the vidscreen, which gradually grew gray once more.

Egg-Or did not concern himself with Exwin's questioning glance. "Mark this well, Exwin: whatever happens, I'm not going to allow any Terrans or Springers from the *Mab* 1 to undergo a brainlash! If the Arkonide spacefleet decides to take matters into its own hands and you learn of it, act as though you were saving your own child from brainlashing! Now, let's see if we can't finally make that call to the Administrator of Soral!"

A few minutes later they had a reply. "The Administrator for the Robot Regent on Soral will not be available for the next 10 days!"

Egg-Or grabbed the microphone for himself. "Then connect me with the chief of defense on Soral, my colleague En-E!"

This time the reply came back sleepily and with half a yawn: "Don't you know it's midnight here? Call back tomorrow morning! Goodby!"

Egg-Or and Exwin swore heartily—then stopped with a start when they heard Sassas giggling.

The positronicon specialist rubbed his hands together in utter delight. "It did me good to hear you gentlemen. We've had more than enough of the Akronides and their structural compensator detector!"

"We didn't say that," said Egg-Or, trying to hold down his anger.

"No," Sassas agreed, "you gentlemen didn't say that." And he winked at them, pleased.

"The general's waiting for your call," Exwin suddenly remembered.

"He'll call here eventually, and when he does, tell him I was called away and you don't know where. If *you* need me or if some important bit of news comes in, I'll be at the *Mab* 1. I want to take a look at those Springers myself."

Egg-Or was driven to the cylindrical spaceship. The broad loading ramp had been connected and on an endless rollband huge quantities of wares and freight rolled out of the starship. But before the first work robot could even touch the merchandise, the cargo had been inspected by 3 different 2-man teams, looking to see if a man might be concealed in the wares.

Egg-Or entered the ship by way of the small ramp in the most forward third. Specialists from the defense ministry were still at work in the com center and the control room. The crew was confined to the main cabin and 1 by 1 at long intervals they were taken in for a renewed interrogation.

The methods used by Egg-Or's men were not brutal. In the long run, however, only especially strong-willed men withstood the psychological techniques.

Face impassive, Egg-Or listened in on the interrogation of a quite young Springer.

According to the youth's own statements, he had been on duty in the Com Center after the 2d transition.

The interrogation took up on this point. Question, answer, question, answer . . . 10 minutes passed and still it was question, answer, question, answer.

20 minutes had gone by. Question, answer, question, answer. Exhaustion had plainly left its mark on the young Springer.

"How did you get the wound on your right hand? Answer me now!"

For the firsttime the galactic trader was taken by surprise. Then he laughed nervously and asked, half ironically: "Where? What wound?" At the same time he looked at his right hand and seemed astonished by what he found. "Where did that come from? It looks bad . . ." he mumbled.

"Who were you fighting with?"

"Me? But I haven't been in a fight for 3 weeks!"

"The wound on your hand is a combat injury! Had you perhaps fought back when the 2d hypercom was being destroyed by a thermobeamer? Who destroyed it? Answer me, Springer!"

"Wait a second . . . Yes, there was something . . . or somebody. But what or who could it have been?"

"You are to answer at once and not waste any more time——"

"Let the man think!" Egg-Or broke in for the firsttime. He had the impression that the young fellow was honestly trying to remember something.

And then Egg-Or suddenly became suspicious. He saw the Springer struggling with his memory; he saw him labor painfully to pull the forgotten out of the past and into the present.

Something's been done to the Springer, Egg-Or thought over & over again and was honestly disappointed when the Springer could not explain where the wound on his hand had come from.

Meanwhile, Exwin, who was responsible for planetary secruity inside the Ent-Than spaceport area, had not been idle. He had requested and received all the available information over the starhell, or Sector 00674 B-00001 as it was officially known, from the archives of the Arkonide Administration on Ekhas. The information he found seemed so important to him that he called his chief at the *Mab* 1.

Egg-Or entered the com center of the cylindrical ship, saw Exwin's face already on the vidscreen and said in a tense voice as he sat down: "Alright, shoot, Exwin!"

Exwin gave a summarized description of the starhell.

"Repeat that again!" Egg-Or suddenly interrupted, bending intently and excitedly closer to the screen.

"Well . . ." the powerful gravity fields and the pure, highly concentrated radiation are capable of disturbing the electrical capacity of the Arkonide nervous system. Staying within Sector 00674 B-00001 for any length of time can result in psychological aberrations of long duration, including depression and paranoia.

"The *Oak-Oak*, a battleship which has since been wrecked, was——"

"I think that's all I need to know," Egg-Or interrupted

Exwin. "This *is* interesting! It explains why the crew seems to know nothing of the whereabouts of the 2 Mabdans. The effects of being in the starhell include not only depressions, baseless fear and so on but also amnesia. But that still doesn't explain where Mabdan 1 and 3 are and who those men were who left the *Mabdan* 1 right after it landed—What is it?" he asked angrily and turned to the side.

One of the hypercom specialists surprised him with the news that the *Mab* 1 had been in radio contact with another spacer while in the starhell.

"Details!" demanded Egg-Or but the scientist only shrugged.

With a reproachful look at the transmitting equipment aboard the cylindrical ship, the scientist explained regretfully: "This old model doesn't have any memory banks for recording incoming and outgoing signals. But the unit that was destroyed by a thermobeam . . . sir, do you know that it's the kind of hypercom found only on the Regent's warships?"

The connection with Exwin was still open and the chief of the spaceport division was listening in. "Sir," he suggested, "why don't I call the planet Soral again and force those sleepy Arkonides at the other end to connect me with the appropriate agency. If the secret service on Soral doesn't know anything about the *Mab* 1, then some other agency must—"

Egg-Or's hand gesture, which betrayed despondency, broke him off. "Exwin, are you still unaware *how* sluggish and irresponsible a *real* Arkonide is? If we can't solve this riddle ourselves, it never will be solved."

"And what if I call the Robot Regent itself, sir?"

Egg-Or laughed. "I won't forbid you but I won't recommend you do it either. If I were you, I wouldn't. Do you seriously believe the Regent has been informed of this trifling matter? Seen in the broad perspective, this affair isn't important at all. The headaches are left to us."

Exwin's face showed dissatisfaction. "Sir, I've set the alien police to looking for 4 to 6 Springers and I mentioned that 1 of them will be seriously ill. But 4 or 6 Springers who arrived with the *Mab* 1 are nowhere to be found. It's enough to drive me to despair."

150 ADVENTURES FROM NOW
You'll see the
Andro-Alpha Abduction

6/ TAKING THE BAIT

Although the upper 5th was taken up with the prison, the Star Of Arkon was Ent-Than's largest hotel.

Perry Rhodan and his 3 mutants found quarters in the vast building's lower third.

They had left the *Mab* 1 just a few minutes after landing without taking any special security precautions. An automatic ground taxi had taken them to an airtaxi stop and from there along with Springers and Arkonides from various other spacers they were taken to the flight-deck on the roof of the Star of Arkon.

They were registered at the front desk and according to their identification and other papers they came from all directions on different spaceships. But not one had arrived with the *Mab* 1.

The 4 Terrans were given quarters on 3 different floors. The mutants were told to meet Perry Rhodan in his room in 30 minutes.

Before Rhodan parted company with Fellmer Lloyd, he had the telepath and sensor attempt to discern the whereabouts of Maj. Clyde Ostal and the crew of the *Tigris* by means of his psychic abilities.

Fellmer Lloyd was quite familiar with Ostal's brain-wave pattern but no matter where he turned, he could not perceive the Major's pattern among the thousands he sensed.

When he entered Perry Rhodan's hotel room half an hour later, Kitai Ishibashi and Tako Kakuta were already present.

Lloyd understood Rhodan's telepathic question. *No,* he replied in the same manner. *I haven't been able to contact them.*

Rhodan looked at him, meditating. He could not forget what he had seen at the spaceport: the merchant ship *Tigris* standing out in the portion of the field reserved exclusively for the Arkonide fleet. All its ramps had been extended and all hatches were wide open.

"Kakuta," Rhodan said to the slender teleporter, whose small figure passed least well for that of a Springer, "I'd very much like to know what's going on now aboard the *Tigris* and if any of the crew are still there. But don't take any risks. Would 10 minutes be enough?"

Kakuta, who like the others was disguised as a Springer, chuckled. "I'll be back right on time, sir!"

Then the air where he was sitting began to shimmer strangely. The energy the small Japanese was now developing within himself allowed him to leave the room and rematerialize in the place he was concentrating on: Maj. Clyde Ostal's cabin aboard the *Tigris.*

Hardly had the teleporter disappeared than Fellmer Lloyd was given his orders.

"Try to find the commanding general in the Arkonide fleet headquarters, Lloyd. We have to find out as soon as we can where Maj. Ostal and his men are. I have the feeling someone is searching for us."

Fellmer Lloyd, leaning back comfortably in his seat, closed his eyes. For him the world consisted only of brainwave patterns, of telepathic energy and his spotting sense. He no longer perceived what Perry Rhodan was now saying to Kitai Ishibashi.

"The crew of the *Mab* 1 is going to make problems for us, Ishibashi. That is not meant as a reproach. I'm able to judge whether or not you've done your work well but if from here on in we don't have enough time for good work, then we'll have to be ready for trouble of any kind. Because of the capture of the *Tigris*, the Ekhonides are going to be uneasy and so doubly distrustful. That means that they'll examine very closely every spaceship that doesn't carry passengers and they'll surely notice that there isn't any captain on board the *Mab 1*."

"I could influence anyone who tries to investigate the *Mab 1* . . ."

"It's too late," Rhodan said. "Because of what happened on it, we arrived here too late. Who knows how many people are already involved with the Springer ship by now and . . ."

Kakuta made his reappearance in a shimmering of air, sitting in his former seat as though he had never left. Rhodan and Ishibashi looked at him expectantly but Fellmer Lloyd saw and heard nothing of what was going on around him.

"Sir," the slender Oriental began. "The control room and Com Center are swarming with scientists from the planetary defense. Their chief is named Egg-Or. I heard the men talking about him. I also heard that they've swallowed our bait whole. They believe that in a few hours they'll have the Earth's coordinates. Not one Ekhonide suspects that all the information they've labored so long to extract is fallacious."

"Did you learn anything about the crew?" Rhodan wanted to know.

"Not a word .Everyone was too busy trying to get their job done. No one spoke of our men."

Rhodan glanced at Fellmer Lloyd but he still sat with his eyes closed, seeming to be listening to something far away.

"Ishibashi, I don't want to underestimate the Ekhonide defense and alien police. Go down to the reception desk in the lobby and put a block on the 5 or 8 Ekhonides I saw on duty there."

"Right, sir," answered the thin suggestor and quietly left the well-furnished hotel room.

He went down by way of the antigrav lift and crossed the huge lobby to the reception desk. Everywhere he saw registrar robots and had the feeling that they were somehow perceiving him, for their staring lens-eyes were trained on him. He went up to the desk, behaving like a traveler who had left his home planet for the firstime and felt lonely and uncertain on this alien world.

Kitai Ishibashi did not force his way through the crowd to the desk but the others did. Springers, Aras, Arkonides and intelligences belonging to non-human races, even some in spacesuits because the local atmosphere was deadly for them—they all pushed and shoved towards the desk, wanting information from the 9 Ekhonides on duty behind the counter.

Kitai Ishibashi heard the stock answer over & over again: "Please direct your question to one of our information robots! Please direct your question to one of . . ."

Kitai Ishibashi did not force his way through the of the strain of his efforts to concentrate his suggestive power and beam it at the Ekhonides behind the desk.

His suggestive order was simple: "Tell any officials who inquire about 4, 5 or 6 Springers that with more than 20,000 guests in your hotel you cannot give any information. Refer them to your information robots!"

It was an order that could not be any simpler and still attempt to protect Perry Rhodan and his 3 mutants.

But Kitai Ishibashi was not through with his work yet.

Suddenly he pushed his way up to the desk. "May I help you, sir?" he was asked by the Ekhonide behind the counter.

"I'd like . . ." Ishibashi began, and thereafter he only moved his lips. Any chance observers would have heard nothing. Using all his power, the mutant suggested to the young Ekhonide: *Tell me when the registrar robots are changed!*

"Only once a year, sir," answered the Ekhonide politely, convinced that the slender Springer had asked the question out loud.

Who gives the order for the robots to be changed? Ishibashi next demanded.

"Ulgald, our chief engineer, sir . . ."

Where can I find him?

"On the 1st floor, wing gg-/3, Registry Dept., sir."

"Thank you," said Ishibashi out loud. He left quickly, then searched for the registry department on the 1st floor. He spoke to an Ekhonide he met on the way and got directions.

"Forget that you ever spoke to a Springer!" Ishibashi ordered suggestively, then went on with his search for chief engineer Ulgald.

But he was not sufficiently familiar with the arrangement of Ekhonide offices in the building and lost his way. He asked directions of another Ekhonide after a long wandering about, and the reply was:

"I am Ulgald, Springer . . ."

As the 2 went to the antigrav lift shaft, as companionable as old friends, the chief engineer seemed no different than usual. He gave the tall, thin galactic trader with the slightly bent posture a hearty farewell, then quickly went off to his office to order a change of robots.

His order was accompanied with a note of such urgency that no refusal or even questioning of his instructions was possible.

The young Ekhonide at the reception desk did not remember Ishibashi or his questioning even while the robots were being changed.

10 minutes before the alien police arrived, the robot change was complete. The memory banks containing information covering the last 9 months and 3 days were completely erased and blank.

Bits of information that might have led to Perry Rhodan and his mutants no longer existed.

For the firsttime in the hotel's history, the Star of Akron had no records concerning its guests. To make the confusion complete, the memory bank erasure had taken place just before the robots were scheduled to transmit their recorded data to the bookkeeping department, as they did regularly every 3 hours.

Ulgald, who would remember this terrible day with a shudder still 20 years later, did not lose his position for the alien police wrote the inconvenient robot change off as an act of pure chance and left, shrugging their shoulders in resignation.

Subjecting every single one of the more than 20,000 guests of the Star of Arkon was beyond even their capabilities.

When Kitai Ishibashi reentered Perry Rhodan's room after a 45 minute absence, Tako Kakuta was already back from his 2d teleportation spring. In the meantime, Fellmer Lloyd had read the thoughts of General Sutokk—and once during the telepathic reception even laughed out loud.

"What?" Perry Rhodan had demanded in surprise, looking at Fellmer Lloyd in disbelief. "Ostal and his men made their escape stark naked? Are you sure the General wasn't telling some disreputable joke while you were reading his mind, Lloyd?"

Fellmer Lloyd swore that the General had not been telling any jokes. In any event, the General had no good thoughts of any sort for the chief of the planetary defense because Egg-Or had refused to allow the Arkonide fleet to brainlash even one solitary Terran.

"But is he trying to make a connection between the *Mab* 1 and the capture of the *Tigris?*" Rhodan pressed.

"He isn't exerting himself especially in that area, sir. He's much more interested in getting Earth's galactic coordinates into his hands as fast as he can."

"He'll have them before long," said Perry Rhodan, half sunk in thought. "Kakuta is taking his time . . ."

The small, slender Oriental had made his 2d spring to the flagship of General Sutokk for a look at the newly developed Compensator Detector.

As a mutant he, like most of his comrades, had not only received a cell renewal on the planet Wanderer to keep him from aging for the next 62 years but again like most of his comrades he had undergone an intensive hypnotraining that made him well-informed in all areas of knowledge.

Tako Kakuta rematerialized in the vast transformer chamber of the flagship *Ebneb,* in the shadow of a housesized, ring-shaped magnetic coil that reached from the floor to the ceiling and angled over the transformer at 45°.

The light noise that Tako Kakuta made by his materialization was drowned out by the constant humming of a large number of energy banks.

Neither the transformer nor the energy banks—huge machines that would have been enough to have supplied a planet of average industrialization with electrical power for 5 years—nor the magnetic coils nor the insulated circuit boards of gigantic dimensions could impress Tako Kakuta. The engine rooms of the *Titan* and the *Drusus* had accustomed him to a larger scale.

He had arrived where he had wanted to go. Arkonide spacebattleships differed from one another about as much as so many eggs; only in the class of ship and in the weaponry could any variation be seen. Kakuta felt as much at home here in the *Ebneb* as he would have aboard the *Lotus,* the *Ganymede* or the *Drusus.*

He saw a metal catwalk winding around the transformer about 3 meters above the floor. He teleported himself up to it, looked out over the circuitry and discovered 2 Ekhonides conversing with one another. They turned their backs to him, sat down on an energy cable, dangled their legs and laughed aloud.

He had to get them out of the transformer chamber or at least to distract them that they would not hear the opening and closing of a diaphragm-like hatch.

Tako Kakuta had no love for radical methods. He always tried to find means that would bring him safely to his goal without having unfortunate consequences for innocent bystanders.

He stood next to the magnet regulator, which could alter the position of the giant magnetic coil. A fleeting smile crossed his face. He grasped the regulator with both hands and under the force of his fingers the wheel turned. The huge coil began to sink from 45° to 30°.

The coil was held floating in place by controlled antigrav fields and as it changed position a positronic warning system sensed that it had sunk too far. A siren screamed out, growing louder the more Tako Kakuta allowed the floating magnetic coil to sink. It was a work of seconds and would have been suicidal for any normal man to attempt, for he would have been seen by the Ekhonides. Since he was a teleporter, however, the place where he had been standing was suddenly empty.

2 frightened Ekhonides raced up the steps to the control board after first having had to run around the transformer.

The alarm still howled. The 2 Ekhonide space soldiers thought only of the punishment awaiting them and so far had not concerned themselves for the reason for the magnetic coil alarm.

Tako Kakuta had performed 2 short teleportations. The last spring brought him to the hatch. Behind it lay the structocomp, an improbably small device in relation to its power.

But the newly developed compensator detector must be here, too. Marshal Allan D. Mercant's scientific staff had at least reasoned as much and they had not been wrong yet in their analyses.

The hatch opened, let the Japanese through and closed again.

Seconds later, Kakuta stood before the great secret.

"So that's the thing that's supposed to bring about our downfall!" he heard himself say. Then his eyes searched for the gray-colored bulges that would unfasten the machinery's covering once he had rested his hand on them.

The compensator detector, about 3 meters high and more than 10 meters long, was connected to the structural compensator located next to it. Tako Kakuta did not think of sabotage. The Chief had not given him any orders for it. Perry Rhodan wanted much more to know the details of the compensator detector's construction.

He laid his hands against 2 bulges in the covering and

a piece of it separated from the rest. Kakuta let it drop to the floor.

The newly developed compensator detector revealed its secrets to the knowing eyes of the Japanese mutant. In the same moment that he had first glimpsed the inner workings of the machinery through the hole in the covering, his entire knowledge of this area of technology had awakened within him.

He gave a start. The construction as displayed in its fundamentals was familiar to him! It reminded him of the pickle people, the Swoons, and at the same time he understood that Arkon's newly developed sensing device was simply an enlarged copy of the Swoonish invention.

An uncanny intimation struck him all at once and he glanced back at the hatch.

As his head turned he concentrated for a teleportion spring behind the structocomp.

The hatch sprang open. A man, one of the 2 Ekhonide space soldiers, started to come in and let out a yell—and then Kakuta saw him no more. His short teleport had brought him behind the structocomp. But he hesitated to disappear completely. He wanted to find out what the Ekhonide would do when he saw that a piece of the detector covering had been removed. Kakuta was fortunate that the Ekhonide was motivated solely by a desire to escape punishment and was thus ready to cover up events he would have otherwise reported.

"Stars and suns!" Kakuta heard him mutter with a trembling voice. "I haven't been drinking any Uquir! I've never believed in ghosts before but I do now. Why, the little stardevils must have taken this plate off the machine . . . !"

Kakuta listened as the Ekhonide replaced the covering, then with the force of his will sprang back to Perry Rhodan's room in the Star of Arkon.

And after him Kitai Ishibashi arrived. Ishibashi had been away the longest but had the least to report.

"Now, where are Ostal and his men?" asked Perry Rhodan.

Fellmer Lloyd looked at him without the faintest idea. "I can't perceive them, sir. If only at least one Ekhonide or even that fleet general knew something . . . but the general is only toying with the notion of giving some Springer a brainlashing."

A dangerous light seemed to appear in Perry Rhodan's eyes. "He won't succeed in that. *We'll* have to see to that but I think we also must be prepared in the event they find our men. Certainly at the moment they aren't feeling any too comfortable. Let's go."

200 ADVENTURES FROM NOW
You'll root for
Flagship in Distress

7/ OF ROCKS & ROBOTS

Egg-Or did not get to bed.

Gen. Sutokk of the Arkonide fleet stationed on Ekhas did not think of sleeping at all.

Perry Rhodan and his 3 mutants were on their way through the night-lit metropolis of Ent-Than, buying clothes for the fugitive Terrans and obtaining a freight transporting vehicle.

Maj. Clyde Ostal and his 32 men were on their way too.

They stood on the edge of a large clearing and saw over the treetops a greenish-lit moon. Over the right side of the clearing was another moon, 3 times larger than the first. It, too, reflected greenish light, so brightly that the opposite forest edge cast shadows and the men could see out over the broad, level expanse.

The forest of the planet Ekhas was silent. Its quiet was uncanny. No night animals called out, neither the birds flying through the darkness nor the mammals who fled at the approach of man.

Nor was there any wind.

But despite the lateness of the night, it was still oppressively humid. The atmosphere was supersaturated with moisture. Sweat gushed out of the pores of all 33 Terrans.

They had been standing under the trees at forest's edge for some minutes. They were waiting for Maj. Ostal to give the order to march on. But not yet. Ostal was inquiring into the cases of 6 men with foot problems. Allan

D. Mercant's rugged training had taught them every-thing—everything except the art of going through a vast, trackless forest barefoot.

All craved water; the thirst had closed their mouths. Only those who absolutely had to speak said anything. They had given up muttering and cursing. But their morale was good.

Whatever they had not attained today would be theirs tomorrow or the next day. Clothes. Food. Water.

Suddenly the larger moon disappeared behind a cloud that had silently crept across the night sky of Ekhas. Now more clouds came and the smaller half moon vanished as well. From a distant wall of black clouds the 33 men heard a thundering and soon after the first lightning was seen crashing to the ground. The thunder grew louder.

"A storm!" the Major cried. "A storm will bring water, men!"

He was promising water both to them and to himself.

But first came the storm and with its howling innum-erable flashes of lightning blasted over the men.

Suddenly the clearing lay in the harsh light of the thundering forces of nature unleashed.

33 men saw the cabin—or the house—simultaneously. Maj. Ostal tried to shout above the chaos but only S. Seeger, who stood next to him, understood what he had said.

Lt. Seeger yelled into the ear of the next man. "Follow us! Pass the order on!"

A long chain of 33 men ran barefoot across the grassy meadow toward the building on the other side.

Then came the rain. It gushed out of the clouds as though from a waterfall.

Large puddles quickly formed on the ground. Even Maj. Ostal took advantage of them to still his thirst. The water was warm and smelled brackish: they only noticed it once they had drunk their fill and wiped their no longer cracked lips with their hands.

"Onwards!" came Ostal's order, which was passed from man to man.

They ran, and the unchained energies in the sky above provided enough light that no one became separated from the rest.

The clearing was wider than they had first estimated in the unfamiliar light of the 2 moons.

And then the storm died just as suddenly as it had arisen.

They had still not reached the cabin or house on the other side of the clearing.

The 2 moons appeared in the sky once more.

All of a sudden the Major signaled with an outstretched arm for the 2 men following him to stop. The order was repeated and everyone in the group quickly came to a halt. No one saw anything; then Seeger and Sgt. Fip heard the Major's order. "You 2 follow me! The others stay here!"

They had been wading by 3s through large pools of water which were already being slowly absorbed by the thirsty ground.

Ostal pointed the direction in which to go and Seeger and Fip silently followed.

Then Ostal held out his arms again and stopped the 2 men. At the same time he made a low hissing noise. He had seen something. Seeger and Fip tried to penetrate the darkness with their eyes.

Isn't that a light? Seeger asked himself just as at his side Fip whispered: "I see a light!"

Against the black background of the forest's edge showed the barely visible form of a low, flat building, lit at one place by the weak light source which the Major had discovered before Fip and Seeger.

Clyde Ostal slowly took cover on the ground. If there were alert observers in the building, then the Terrans, standing out in the full light of the 2 moons, had just been seen. Lt. Seeger and Sgt. Fip followed the example of their superior, then crawled on their stomachs to the right and to the left so that in case of attack the small party would not be wiped out by a single shot.

"Seeger, come with me!" Ostal ordered. "Fip, you try to get back to the men if anything happens to us. Under no circumstances are you to try to help us. It would be senseless in the situation we're in now. Fip, I'm counting on you!"

Ostal and Seeger approached the building from the right, running stooped and in a wide, curving path. In that fashion they reached the dark shadows of the forest's edge and there dared to continue in an upright position.

Maj. Clyde Ostal was about 6 meters ahead of his lieutenant. Before him the outlines of the flat building became ever sharper. It was not a simple cabin but a building made of plastic, the plastic Arkonides had used for construction of houses for millenniums.

Suddenly Ostal stopped as though rooted to the spot. Next to the left corner of the building, the one turned to the clearing, he saw the outline of a robot. "Back, Seeger!" was all he could say before a powerful hypnobeam struck him and he lost consciousness.

Lt. S. Seeger was not a victim of panic. The word did not exist in Allan D. Mercant's training. He reacted unbelievably fast. He watched as the robot strode out of the shadowed side of the building, went to its victim, bent down and picked him up—then he watched as the robot carried Maj. Ostal to the low building.

During his observation Seeger had crawled back into the shadows of the woods. He did not understand why the mechanical man had not detected him and put him out of action, too.

As carefully and cautiously as he could, Seeger made his way back to Sgt. Fip. When he saw the lieutenant was alone, Fip whispered: "What happened to the major?"

"Robots back there!" was the lieutenant's reply and Fip did not need to inquire any further.

When they returned to the waiting group, Lt. Seeger took over the leadership. They marched onward across the clearing, avoiding the building by going far to the left of it, reached the forest and continued from there.

In Terran measurements, a full day on Ekhas lasted 38 hours. They had fought through the night and forest for 10 hours, and 9 hours of darkness still stretched before them. They were too realistic to have any hope of coming to a settlement by daybreak. The day before they had seen no human communities from the airtaxi high above the forest. So it struck them as a completely unexpected surprise when they spotted some dozen unmoving lights shining through the trees ahead.

"Sgt. Fip!" Lt. Seeger said, calling the man to him. "The 2 of us will . . ."

The night stillness was torn by the typical thunder of spaceship engines.

"On to the forest edge!" Seeger ordered.

But they did not reach any forest's edge. The forest simply petered out into a downsloping terrain covered by tall bushes. In front of them, lit by the greenish radiance of the 2 moons, stretched a kilometer-wide band of tangled shrubs and creeping vines that at first steeply then gradually descended to merge into the plain below.

"No wonder we didn't see *that* from the airtaxi," said Lt. Peter H. Hasting, looking out across to the distant lights, and listening, like all the others, to the increasing roar of engines. "But that out there can't possibly be the spaceport of Ent-Than." Then he noticed something about his own body: the arm he had extended for pointing across the plain had been broken—now it was healed!

The claims of the Ekhonide prison doctors had been proven true. The new Ara treatment, a serum that had been injected into his arm, had accomplished the healing process in less than 20 hours. The preparations used up to now in the Great Imperium, also known and used in Perry Rhodan's Solar Imperium, required 50 to 60 hours to take full effect.

Lt. Hasting wanted to bring it to the attention of his comrades but at that moment a cylindrical spaceship took off, silhouetted against the once more clear night sky. At first it rose almost straight up but at 500 meters leveled off for horizontal flight that would take it directly over the Terrans' heads.

Engines roaring, it sped past them and for half a minute thereafter a ringing, distant thunder was the last to be heard from it.

"The lights . . ." Lt. Seeger exclaimed and pointed in the distance.

One light after another went out. Then the brushland before them lay as though it were virgin, untouched wilderness.

"And our major . . ." It could not be determined who said that but it was said and the words had the effect of an exploding bomb. 32 men were suddenly ashamed. They had left Ostal to his fate without even lifting a finger to help him.

Seeger whirled around. "I don't care to know who just

said that but I must remind you just what sort of situation we're now in." His voice had a sharp edge to it. "We have not deserted the major. He ordered us not to do anything if something happened to him or me or both of us. And we can do something to find and help him only when we have the means to do it. I think we can find those means where the Springer ship took off from, there where the lights were burning. We have to get there before daylight. We *must* do it, men!"

They did it but not before daybreak.

Seeger, Hasting and Fip stood before the last bushes and cautiously drew the branches aside.

50 feet ahead, 3 Springer robots stood like steel monuments. The light from yellow star Naral reflected off their optical lenses. It did not bother the robots: positronic systems are not so easily blinded.

Now one of the robots turned in the direction of the Terrans. Fip was last to let go of the branch he was holding. The men stood unmoving. They knew that Springer robots were not as sensitive or as perceptive as Arkonide robots. All their hope rested in that fact.

5 long minutes ticked by. There was neither the hollow tread of an approaching robot nor the low hissing of a thermobeam slicing into their hiding place.

"We can't stand here forever!" Peter Hasting whispered. "How can I go talk to a Springer without being blasted by a robot in the attempt?"

"Hasting," said Seeger, "how do you hope to find a Springer to talk to when we don't even see a single building here? Only the robots are any kind of hint that there's something here . . . What can you make of that?"

"Everything, Seeger. Whoever sneaks into this wilderness is attempting to hide something from the Ekhonides. And whoever has something to hide is not necessarily our enemy. And if we warn the Springers that we were . . . ." He gave a start and asked hastily: "Could the low building with the weak light and the robot guard belong to the same Springer clan? Seeger, Fip . . . what do you think?"

Seeger shook his head. "The low building stood unhidden on the edge of the clearing. It can be clearly seen from above. But here there seems to be hidden an actual landing place for spaceships. I don't see any connection between this place and the building where the major was taken prisoner."

"If that's true, it reinforces my position," said Hasting without further comment on the matter. "Seeger, 3 or 4 men have to take some risks now. We have only stones at our disposal. I need men who are good at throwing stones and hitting their targets . . . Allan D. Mercant, that's something you never taught us in your commando school: throwing stones at positronic robots!"

Lt. Seeger laid his hand on his comrade's shoulder. "And what will *you* be doing while the robots are distracted by the hail of stones?" he asked, his expression sharply suspicious.

Peter Hasting replied: "Well, *one* of us has to try it. When the robots are distracted, I'll make a break for it."

"No!" Seeger exclaimed energetically. "That'd be suicide!"

"Do you know any other solution, Seeger?" asked Hasting calmly.

"Let me go in your place, Lt. Hasting!" offered Sgt. Fip.

"It's 2 against 1," said Hasting with a grateful glance at Fip. "The sergeant also sees that my plan has a chance. Will you give the orders for it? Once the first stones fall and the robots take a closer look, I'll make my dash. But see to it that I have the most possible freedom of movement on the right side. The bushes are thickest there. Well . . .?"

Lt. Seeger was still not happy with his comrade's plan and had he known that Hasting himself reckoned the chance of success at 3%, he would never have relented.

Reluctantly he nodded his agreement and silently disappeared behind the thick 4-meter high bushes.

Peter Hasting lay poised, ready to spring. By now, he figured, Lt. Seeger must have finished with his preparations.

Then he saw on the right 6, 7 or 8 fist-sized rocks flying soundlessly through the air. Just above him a 2d flight of stones whizzed towards the robot standing in the middle.

The stones thudded into the ground near where the robot stood. Through a narrow gap in the protective bushes Hasting saw the middle and rightward robots turn around, and the ponderous step of the robots mixed with the thudding of fist-sized stones.

The men Seeger had put on this operation threw their stones almost unceasingly.

Then the rightmost robot reacted with its deadly weaponry.

3 beams hissed in the bright morning light and annihilated a portion of the onflying rocks. The robot Hasting had been standing precisely in front of reacted the same way, having moved somewhat to the left.

The moment had come for Hasting to make his break!

The optical lens systems of the robots stared at the rock swarms coming at them. Hasting knew that the robots could not "see" behind themselves. But he also knew that the robots would find out in a few seconds the place from which the stones were coming and train all their ray weapons on it, not letting up with their fire until the ground was bubbling lava.

The gap between the 2 robots on the right and in front of him was not even 100 meters. Peter Hasting ran like he had never run before. He constantly looked in both directions. The 2 battle machines were about 3/4ths turned away from him but only a slight turn would be enough to bring him into their field of vision.

Instinctively he threw himself under a bush at a full run but he did not remain where he was. He crawled farther, like an Indian, and managed not to touch a single one of the low-hanging branches.

Then he heard 2 sharp impacts in rapid succession. 2 stones had struck a robot about to turn in his direction.

Hasting considered with forceful logic.

Positronic brains were unfeeling. Being hit with stones did not bother them but the impact was only the beginning of an attack and therefore the robot must react to it and turn back to where it was.

Hasting sprang up again, threw himself between 2 bushes, losing the robots from view in the process, and then was shocked to see a ray hit the ground 3 meters in front of him. The ground began to melt.

The robot on the left had spotted him!

Hasting turned, wanting to run back in his first reaction, then through a gap in the branches he saw 2 Springers running toward him, summoned out of their quietude by the robot alarm.

Hands raised above his head, Peter H. Hasting ran towards them.

Behind his back, a new impulse beam was fired by one of the robots and this time only missed him by a hair.

The heat from the bushes and earth blasted into gas struck him all over the surface of his back.

2 uncomprehending Springers let their weapons sink!

The naked man running towards them with his hands raised could be judged harmless with one glance.

250 ADVENTURES FROM NOW
You'll witness the
Incident in Tiger Sector

8/ THE COSMICAVALRY COMES THRU!

Egg-Or not only looked up in surprise when the 2 robots brought Maj. Clyde Ostal into his office—he leaped out of his chair and started at the Terran.

They knew each other!

And the Terran's mocking expression bothered the chief of planetary defense for Ekhas more than he was willing to admit.

"Sit down, Terran!" snapped Egg-Or more sharply than he had intended.

A mocking look faced him again and Maj. Clyde Ostal asked: "Do Terrans have the effect of ghosts on Ekhonides and Arkonides or was it only your guilty conscience that got you up out of your seat?"

Against his will, Egg-Or was impressed by the fearlessness of the man with the impassive face.

"Sit down . . . please!" The "please" came after a conspicuous pause.

Clyde Ostal glanced at the Robots on either side. "Will these gentlemen object, Ekhonide?"

"You're making it difficult for me to speak reasonably with you," said Egg-Or.

"Give me my *Tigris* back, let me have my crew and allow me to take off with my spacer. Then we'll be able to talk over the hypercom like good friends," said Clyde Ostal, business-like. "Thereafter I would be happy to report to Perry Rhodan that on Ekhas there's at least one decent Ekhonide."

"I'd like to know what gives you your confidence, Terran. Your Perry Rhodan won't help you . . ." The Terran's mocking smile confused him. Frightened, Egg-Or thought of the general's suspicion that Perry Rhodan had only been setting out a decoy with the *Tigris*.

"Rhodan?" asked Clyde Ostal, surprised. "Ekhonide, who do you think we Terrans are? Each one of us is a Perry Rhodan! All of us! How long will it take for the Great Imperium to finally learn *that?* We don't sleep with our eyes open but we do play with open cards and . . . Ekhonide, we're looking for friends so that we can live with our friends in peace!"

The call from Gen. Sutokk interrupted the conversation between Egg-Or and Ostal just as it was beginning to enter an interesting phase. On the vidscreen appeared Sutokk's harshly outlined face. His voice was equally as harsh. "Egg-Or, I have just learned that the captain of that merchant was recaptured. I request that you turn him over to the Arkonide fleet immediately. By order of the Regent! You'll have the original of that order in the next 10 minutes! Over & out!"

Did this Egg-Or forget about me? Clyde Ostal wondered, looking at the Ekhonide who stared without seeing at the graying vidscreen. Ostal was still standing in front of Egg-Or's desk, flanked by the 2 Arkonide robots. Then Ostal's distrust awakened. Why had this Gen. Sutokk emphasized that it was an order of the Regent for the Terran to be turned over to the fleet and that the original of the order would shortly be sent over to Egg-Or?

Was there some sort of rivalry between Egg-Or and the General?

In that same moment, Fellmer Lloyd impulsively laid his hand on the arm of the Administrator of the Solar

Imperium. They sat by 2s at different tables, waiting in the predominantly Springer-trade restaurant for the rollband to bring their orders to the table.

"I'm on Ostal's trail, Chief," whispered Lloyd from behind his hand and then switched to the telepathic connection.

Clyde Ostal now finds himself a prisoner of Egg-Or. This Sutokk seems to be an especially fanatical supporter of brainlashing, for his orders are that Ostal is to go into brainlash as soon as he is delivered . . . Egg-Or, chief of the planetary defense, has so far refused to allow any Terran or Springer from the Mab 1 to be turned over to the fleet for a brainlash . . . Chief, there's even an order from the Robot Regent demanding brainlashing. The original of the order has just been delivered to Egg-Or by courier . . . Odd. They're only thinking of Major Ostal. The General hasn't thought once about the rest of the Tigris crew . . .

"Well," said Perry Rhodan in a low voice, seeming to regard with interest the food on the dishes just delivered by the rollband. "Soup's on!"

"OK, I see . . ." Fellmer Lloyd said without thinking, receiving Rhodan's telepathic order:

You must now find Clyde Ostal, Lloyd! Search for him; then I can put Kakuta and Ishibashi into action. If I understand your thoughts correctly, Ostal must be in the city. Why is it so hard for you to find him now?

For Fellmer Lloyd there was only one answer to that: *Ostal isn't thinking of us at all, Chief! I don't believe he thinks we're on Ekhas. There isn't any other explanation. If he would only wish we were here one single time . . .* Fellmer Lloyd's thoughts suddenly broke, as though his mind had suddenly gone mute. Then his thoughts hammered against Rhodan's forehead once more: *Chief, a swarm of officials from the alien police are on their way here to investigate the place!*

Among the thousand or more Springers in the restaurant, their getting up and motioning Ishibashi and Kakuta to follow did not attract any attention. They headed by pairs towards the 4 rear exits.

On the way, Lloyd came close to Ishibashi briefly, long enough to whisper in English to him: "Alien police are coming to investigate here!"

"Surely we didn't have to leave our food in the lurch like this," Ishibashi commented in Interkosmo.

"Orders from the Chief," Fellmer Lloyd whispered back in answer and separated himself unobtrusively from the other mutants, going towards the 3d rear exit with Rhodan. There they found that the alien police had arrived first. The officials in their inconspicuous uniforms occupied all the rear exits. From this moment on, no guest could leave the restaurant without having his papers checked.

With the calm of a genuine Springer, Perry Rhodan gave up his identification pass, which had been manufactured by Solar Defense. The official who was to check him gave it back after a fleeting glance. Fellmer Lloyd experienced the same.

They crossed the street by way of a bridge-like antigravity band. In front of them floated Tako Kakuta and Kitai Ishibashi.

"Well done, Ishibashi," said Rhodan as he and Lloyd caught up with them.

At that moment Fellmer Lloyd lost contact with his immediate surroundings. "I've got him, Chief!" Lloyd suddenly exclaimed, slightly exhausted. "He thought of you. He's just learned . . . learned through Egg-Or, that the general wants to have him brought in for brainlashing. The Major is now in the headquarters of planetary defense. He's still in Egg-Or's office, guarded by 2 robots."

"How is it that he was captured alone? Where are his men?" Rhodan suddenly demanded of Lloyd.

Fellmer Lloyd switched again to the telepathic connection, for that means precluded any misunderstandings.

Last night, on a march through the jungle, Ostal and his men discovered an Ekhonide relay station. Ostal approached it alone and was shockbeamed by a robot. The relay serves as a listening post over hypercom communications and it reported its capture to the defense ministry immediately. Ostal was picked up this morning by a small rayship and brought to Egg-Or. Ostal does not know where his men are now.

"Klot!" exclaimed Lt. Seeger, leaping in fright to one side. The face of a slender galactic trader had just suddenly appeared out of nowhere next to him. Then the lieutenant's eyes became unnaturally large and he whispered hoarsely, half in disbelief and half in hope: "Kakuta . . . ?"

Kakuta saved himself the trouble of replying. "What kind of place is this, Seeger?"

With an all-inclusive gesture, the lieutenant indicated the windowless room in which he and 31 men had been imprisoned. "A landing station and trading post for smuggling Springers, and our 2d prison on Ekhas. The Star of Arkon was much more luxurious in comparison . . ."

The teleporter interrupted him, paying no heed to the fact that the entire crew of the *Tigris* had crowded around him in order not to miss a single word. "Is Lt. Hasting still dickering with the Springers?"

Lt. Seeger repressed his surprise at Kakuta's excellent information and hastened to reply: "They've been at it for hours. Or we hope they're still at it, anyway, and that they just didn't lock him up by himself somewhere. Tough customers, these Springers! Well, at least we have clothes now and we've had something to eat . . ."

"Describe to me the room in which Hasting is conferring with the Springers! Are you familiar with it, Lieutenant?"

"Yes, I was in there for 10 minutes myself. It's underground, too, only a lot deeper than this hole. If I'm not mistaken, 2 or 3 large storerooms lay behind it. The room looks as follows . . ." And with astounding precision he described the parley room in a few words but so graphically that the teleporter Tako Kakuta could picture it well in his own mind.

The mutant disappeared in a shimmering of air, as silently as he had come.

Tako Kakuta rematerialized in total darkness. The numbing aroma of unknown herbs or drugs penetrated his nose like a cloud of poison gas. He thought of Lt. Seeger's assertion that there were 2 or 3 of these storerooms below the ground.

His teleportation succeeded. He rematerialized in halfway fresh air, though again in impenetrable darkness. He looked around for a moment but found no light anywhere and switched on his spotlight.

The spotlight had been built into the 3d button of his overalls and represented a piece of Swoon work. While Allan D. Mercant's Solar Defense had not yet been equipped with Swoon devices, Rhodan's mutant corps had already been outfitted completely with the unbelievably tiny but monstrously powerful and maintenance-free gadgets.

The beam of his spotlight rested on the large storeroom door. Nowhere could Kakuta find an energy barrier or an alarm system. Calmly he threaded his way between the piles of merchandise crates to the door.

The door could be opened. The teleporter pushed it open only as far as a hand's breadth and peered through the slit. Kakuta was looking into the very room that Lt. Seeger had so precisely described to him. Voices came to his ear, speaking in the plainest of Interkosmo. Now he recognized the voice of Lt. Peter Hasting. There was impatience in his tone and a threat.

"Springers . . . for the lastime! Help us and you'll make the best bargain of your lives! It'll be all over for smuggling drugs, of course, but you'll smuggle information! Valuable information that would interest Perry Rhodan and you'll get good money for it—more money than you're making with smuggling drugs.

"Change your smuggling operation into a secret information agency. It surely won't be hard for you to do it. And don't tell me how much you're concerned with the security of the Imperium! You must make your choice . . . now! And if you decide for Rhodan that means you will secure a spaceship for us Terrans at the same time . . ."

"Not so fast, Terran!" Kakuta heard the bass voice of a Springer. "Who's paying for this? You know of course that we can perhaps be the best of friends if you pay better than Arkon or the Aras or whoever."

"Upon my honor as an officer of Perry Rhodan, I promise that payment of the still to be negotiated sum will be made to you 15 days after our escape from Ekhas . . ."

2 or 3 Springers laughed hollowly. Only the trader with the bass voice rumbled: "Shut your mouths, you blithering fools! Didn't you hear what was just said? So you're an officer, eh Terran? Good! Let's talk about what

the spacer will cost and then you can give us your word as Rhodan's officer. I think that will make a very good start . . ."

2 sharply protesting voices loudly interrupted.

"I won't let my clan move a finger for this Terran!" exclaimed one.

"I'm not one bit in support of this Perry Rhodan!" asserted the other.

"Have it any way you like," commented the bass-voiced trader. "We'll just close the deal without you but because you know too much already, you'll just have to make yourself useful on the Gango plantations and . . ."

"What?" shrilly demanded one of the other voices. "Are you threatening us? You want to send us to the drug farms on Klinu-Lun's Planet?"

"You heard me correctly," affirmed the bass-voiced Springer. "Haven't you had enough of this vile drug business? Sooner or later the Ekhonides will spot one of our drug ships taking off or landing . . . and then it will be all up for us!"

Tako Kakuta remained motionless at the slightly opened storeroom door, listening. Hasting's idea of making information agents out of drug-smuggling Springers was worth as much as the peaceful conquest of a planet.

The argument between the Springers went on for half an hour, coming to a sudden end with an ultimatum from the galactic trader who believed implicitly in Lt. Hasting's sworn word. Kakuta did not dare to open the door any farther but he believed that the bass-voiced Springer had made coming to a decision easier for the other 2 by holding a beamer on them.

Suddenly the teleporter heard an inarticulate short cry. His sharp hearing perceived approaching footsteps.

In the same instant he concentrated and as the door behind which he had been listening was jerked open, he teleported back into the first storeroom.

He did not dare breathe the narcotic atmosphere but then came the moment when his lungs were screaming for air. An audacious idea shot through his mind and he carried it out almost simultaneously.

Lt. Hasting saw the air shimmer before him. He did not quite understand what was happening until Tako Kakuta stood in front of him with a thoroughly unfamiliar face. Yet he recognized Kakuta by his small, slender figure and by his manner of entry.

He reacted immediately. He stepped between the Oriental and the Springers, who were busy in the storeroom, blocking their view of him. Kakuta spoke. "Rhodan is on Ekhas. If the *Tigris* crew can't escape with the help of these Springers, we'll get you out of this ourselves. Try to convince the traders that they should become our agents and . . ."

"Disappear, Kakuta!" Hasting hissed at him. He listened to the Springers discuss the open-standing door; they seemed to be looking for something in the storeroom.

2 of the traders saw nothing more than a slight shimmering in the air but thought nothing more of it, chalking the apparition up as an effect of the lighting.

Tako Kakuta rematerialized on the edge of the city where Perry Rhodan, Kitai Ishibashi and Fellmer Lloyd were waiting for him. They stood in front of their small transport vehicle which they had purchased the evening before and which was only partially loaded.

A smile seemed to twinkle in Rhodan's gray eyes. Kakuta had ended his report and Rhodan asked: "I wonder if the police or the planetary defense will ever figure out who these clothes were meant for when they find the truck here with its load today or tomorrow?"

Egg-Or, chief of planetary defense for Ekhas, let Gen. Sutokk's mixed squad of space soldiers wait. Sutokk had ordered over the telescreen for the Terran Clyde Ostal to be turned over to him immediately.

Again flanked by 2 robots, the Major of the Solar Security Service entered. Egg-Or's deathly pale face boded nothing good.

The vidscreen buzzed and a face appeared on it. Ex-win, responsible for the security of the Ent-Than spaceport, spoke hurriedly. "Sir, the Terran crew was spotted at the northern edge of the spaceport when they were leaving a small Springer cutter. But our agent was unable to determine if they boarded a Springer spacer or flew to the city in 3 or 4 airtaxis; he was knocked out by an unknown assailant during the Terrans' disembarking maneuvers. I immediately . . ." For some seconds Ex-win's voice could not be heard. Egg-Or stared at the vidscreen. Maj. Ostal listened with feverish tension.

When & where had his men made contact with Springers and how had they been able to convince these galactic traders to help them?

Now Exwin's voice sounded again from the loud-speaker. "Sir, Gen. Sutokk's space soldiers have also taken up the search for the Terran merchant crew as of just a few minutes ago! The General demanded that I issue an order forbidding all ships from taking off . . . for an unlimited duration! When I refused he threatened me with his fleet."

"Do what he wants, then," said Egg-Or, oddly calm. "But if he gives you any new orders, let me know first before you carry them out. Over & out."

He glanced up and looked at Ostal. "Take a seat if you will, Terran. This may take awhile. I have some things to take care of yet."

Then he remembered the watch robots and sent them out. He watched them go until the door had closed behind them.

Maj. Clyde Ostal sat down hesitantly. He had to admit to himself that he did not know the defense chief very well. Was this Ekhonide simply a declared opponent of brainlashing or was he one of those influential men who in their actions resisted the rule of the positronic Regent on Arkon 3 though through wisdom never displaying their resistance in any revolutionary form?

"Terran," Egg-Or began, forgetting about all the things he was to take care of, "you told me in our last interview that every Terran is a Perry Rhodan. I'm giving you the opportunity to prove it!

"Look here . . ."

Then the telescreen sounded again. Exwin was at the other end. "Sir! Gen. Sutokk's space troops have captured the Terran crew without a fight!"

"Where?" Egg-Or demanded.

"In the headquarters of the United Small Traders on the north edge of the city."

"In the headquarters of the United Small Traders on the north edge of the city," Egg-Or repeated softly, not realizing he had said it out loud. He considered only what he might still do and did not sense the alien force overpowering his thoughts.

Egg-Or suddenly stood up. "Terran, from this moment on it would be senseless to ignore the orders of the Regent. Whatever you and your men have to hide the General will soon know. Meanwhile, Arkon is already aware of Earth's galactic position. Yes, in spite of your erasure of the *Tigris'* positronicon memory banks, we were able to obtain enough data to indicate the place where Terra might be found.

"But just tell me one thing which interests the General and me considerably: was Perry Rhodan behind this puzzling mistransition of your ship?"

Ostal managed a sympathetic smile. "Egg-Or, the *Tigris* is a small merchant vessel and not a ship in the Terran spacefleet. What is so mysterious about the mistransition of my ship, really? Doesn't it happen to every spacer now & then? Or do you have something to hide? It almost seems that way to me, Ekhonide."

"What do you mean by that, Terran?"

"What do I mean? Well, the crime of illegally capturing the *Tigris* is hardly enough for a Gen. Sutokk to make a murderer out of himself as well by ordering members of my crew to undergo a brainlashing! Behind this murderous order is hidden much more . . . but what, Egg-Or? That is what I'm asking myself and what I'm asking *you!*"

Unnoticed by Egg-Or but evident to Maj. Ostal, officer of the Solar Security Service, an astounding change came over the Ekhonide defense chief. His tense face relaxed and a pleasant and friendly Ekhonide made his appearance, nodding affably to Ostal.

Rhodan's here! the Major thought. *One of the mutants is at work on Egg-Or with hypnotic or suggestive power. The cavalry certainly arrived at the last minute this time!*

Egg-Or was chatting now but mentioned nothing of the *Tigris*, Gen. Sutokk or anything else relating to the *Tigris* operation. Then he stood up and approached Ostal, who instinctively rose as well, reached out his hand and said: "You are free to go now. Come visit me again, Ostal, should your travels bring you back to Ekhas. I would be very happy to see you again . . ."

... *though I rather doubt it,* the Major thought as he stepped out onto the street. He was not at all surprised when a small, slender Springer hurried past and whispered to him in English: "Maj. Ostal, go to the head of the 3d street on the right!" The "Springer" went on and after a few steps was lost in the press of the crowd.

400 ADVENTURES FROM NOW
Beware! for
Death Flies Aboard!

9/ THE DESPERATE GAME ENDS

Gen. Sutokk had assembled his staff around him. The newscaster ran constantly, broadcasting one report after the other. All the news was coming from the offices of the United Small Traders. That was a union of small Springer clans who conducted their business together on many different worlds, thus keeping their overhead low. Considered as a single entity, the UST was no small economic factor and the tirading General was reminded of that by an adjutant.

"General, we should let the matter drop. If it should also become known that the Arkon Defense interfered with the strict rank-ordering laws of the Springers in the case of the *Mab* 1, we'd drive a large number of Springer clans straight into Rhodan's arms. The Terran agents are already spreading it quietly around that the Positronicon on Arkon 3 can't be trusted. So I urgently advise that we accept at face value the claim of the Springers in the United Small Traders' offices that the crew of the *Tigris* came in only by chance. We'll find out the truth when we get the Terrans under a brainlash."

Gen. Sutokk finally realized that his adjutant's suggestion was reasonable and would save him a great deal of trouble. With a grim expression he turned to the officer at the newscaster. "Have the Terrans sent to headquarters at once! Should we send out watch robots? . . . What for? 50 men would be enough to safely bring that weaponless group here. Pass on the order, then! What are you waiting for?"

In spite of his success, the General's mood was still bad. He simply could not rid himself of the feeling that Perry Rhodan could be behind the mistransition of the *Tigris*. Moreover, just an hour before his scientists had reported their thoughts on the coordinates obtained from the *Tigris* positronicon.

"General, it's possible that the whole lot of data is false. With the help of the great Arkon Star Catalog we checked out the galactic coordinates and while we did find a solar system in that position, it's a system that has been known to us for 8000 years and contains no inhabited planets."

"You're just now telling me this?" Gen. Sutokk had stormed. "You know that I've already passed the data on to the Regent by hypercom. Have Arkonide ships started flying out to that system yet, gentlemen?"

"So far as we can ascertain, sir, no."

"Then the catalog's wrong!" With that rather audacious statement he had sent the scientists away. He thought of it again as his order was transmitted to the office of the UST for the Terrans to be brought to fleet headquarters, which was located in that part of the spaceport reserved for the Regent's battleships.

The streets leading past the business offices were completely blocked off, resulting in 2 enormous traffic jams. Hundreds of Ekhonides and vehicles grew in minutes to thousands. The civilians were ill-pleased by the stoppage and Arkon's space soldiers suffered all manner of insults.

Then the Ekhonides saw the 30 Terrans whose picture had been continuously broadcast over the television channels since the day before, the same Terrans who had accomplished the impossible by breaking out of the Star of Arkon.

No one paid any attention to 2 galactic traders wedged in the crowd and looking across the street to the Springer trading office door. 1 was small and slender, the other tall and lanky with a slight slouch in his posture. They did not speak. They only saw.

3 armored vehicles pulled up from the side streets. A cordon of heavily-armed space soldiers formed a narrow lane to the armored cars for the Terrans.

The tall, lanky Springer gazed calmly at the loading site. Nothing about him betrayed the vast powers he controlled.

Then the officer wearing a portable communicator, in direct contact with the newscaster in Gen. Sutokk's office, declared the leading operation finished and announced that the 32 Terrans would arrive in the next half hour.

Then the order came for the space soldiers blocking the street from both sides to climb aboard the armored vehicles.

A minute later the convoy rolled out. Nothing more could be seen of the Terrans inside the vehicles.

Traffic moved again and the Ekhonides and tourists could go on their way. The 2 Springers who had stood silently next to each other entered the nearest building.

In the middle of an empty floor, the tall man stood behind the short one, wrapped his arms about his companion's chest—and the air shimmered and the room was suddenly emptier than before.

Out in front of the reception building at the spaceport, 2 Springers stood on the street seeming to wait for something in particular. Their patience was not put to any great test. A small modern truck rolled up and stopped near them. They climbed inside without a word and the man at the throttle, a Springer with a steely gaze, set the truck in motion once more. He drove up to a fork in the road: an unmistakable sign read to the effect that the sideroad led to the headquarters of the Arkonide fleet.

4 Springers sat in the somewhat cramped cab of the truck along with a man who could be recognized at first glance as a Terran: Maj. Clyde Ostal.

They were all waiting for the crew of the *Tigris*.

From their parking place they could see the Terran merchant spacer. Its name shone clearly in the light from Naral reflecting off the surface of the sphere: *Tigris*.

"They're coming," a Springer with Fellmer Lloyd's voice said suddenly. "They're driving at top speed. Everything seems to be running smoothly."

Then the convoy thundered past them but it did not turn in to the sideroad leading to Arkonide Fleet Headquarters. It went straight on!

The small truck started up again and sped up, maintaining a position just behind the armored transports. The group raced past the huge reception and administration building. Now the convoy went out on the spacefield itself, streaking across the flat plasticoncrete surface of the spaceport towards a small Ekhonide spaceship whose crew came out to meet it and seemed to think nothing of leaving a spaceship behind with the engines running and no one aboard.

The armored cars rolled up to the broad ramp leading up into the spacer. The space soldiers sprang out, again forming a double line to make a pathway for the 32 Terrans to reach the alien spaceship. They did not concern themselves with the truck that had held close to the rear armored car nor did they take notice of the 5 men who pushed through the line of guards to climb into the Ekhonide ship too.

In front of the 2d transport vehicle stood an officer making his report over the audio-video communicator.

"In 3 minutes the convoy will turn back towards headquarters. ETA: 15:67 and . . ."

A high-pitched voice bellowed out of the loudspeaker. "What did you say, Thur-Ges? Why did you stop in front of a spaceship? What's going on over there? Answer me!"

With incredible calmness Thur-Ges, officer in the spacefleet of the Regent of Arkon, repeated his statements. "In 3 minutes the convoy will turn back towards headquarters. ETA . . ."

The last Terran to enter the hatch of the small Ekhonide spacer heard the scream from headquarters: "All ships take off immediately! Alarm! Take off immediately! Details will follow!"

Sgt. Fip had been the last man. He closed the hatch and the ramp automatically drew itself in. Meanwhile, Perry Rhodan, at the head of their men, ran through the ship to the control room.

Every second was precious. The lead they had over the Arkonide fleet was only relative. They did not know how many ships the headquarters had already underway in the Naral System.

Perry Rhodan threw himself into the pilot's seat.

Kitai Ishibashi, the suggestor, had once more accomplished an excellent piece of work. All the equipment aboard this small spacer could be immediately turned on at full power. Just then a light came on indicating that all the hatches were closed.

Syncontrol set at "1"!

The engines began to howl.

Antigrav field: max!

The spacer leaped into the blue Ekhonide sky and accelerated like it never had before. The absorber hummed as it soaked up the inertial force of acceleration before it could affect the crew.

"Hypercom ready?" Rhodan asked over the intercom to the Com Center, which on this small ship was adjacent to the control room.

"Ready, Chief," the man at the hypercom unit called back. The word "chief" sounded like a fanfare.

"Prepare a hypercom message for the *Lotus*: Arkon, Arkon . . . No, not that!" Rhodan decided, remembering suddenly that he had already used the word "Arkon" in the middle of the Milky Way for the call from the *Lotus* to the *Mab* 1. "Use this instead: Mercant, Mercant, Mercant . . ."

"Chief . . . ?"

Rhodan already knew what the man at the hypercom wanted to say. "Pronounce it with an Arkonide accent: that's all that's necessary. Then the boys listening in on the 'other side' will have their work cut out for them, trying to figure out what that word repeated 3 times can possibly mean . . ."

The small radar also functioned. The man posted at it reported: "Sir, a battleship is nearing Ekhas. Position . . ." and gave its coordinates.

"I've got him," said Kitai Ishibashi with uncanny calm, meaning the commander of the oncoming Arkonide battlespacer.

Just as he had influenced Egg-Or, 50 Arkonide soldiers and the crew of this small ship, so now he reached across a gigantic distance in space and forced the mind of the enemy commander to his will. 10 minutes later Gen. Sutokk was overcome by a 3d outburst of rage because his radarman reported that the Arkonide spacer had taken a different direction than the one ordered over the radio.

"Has everyone gone crazy?!" he exploded.

Meanwhile the small Ekhonide ship had left the atmosphere. Mercilessly Rhodan drained the ship of everything that it was capable of. Every second was precious. If the Arkonide spacers lying at the spaceport had already taken off, their desperate game would soon be at an end. His suggestor Kitai Ishibashi was no magician and, no matter how much he was capable of, Rhodan knew where his mutant's limits lay.

"Transmit hypercom message!" he called to the Com Center, using his raised voice instead of the intercom as he was even then attempting to raise the small hangar on the latter.

"Fellmer Lloyd?" was all he asked over the intercom.

"Lifeboard ready, Chief. The crew's getting in now."

"Thank you!" Rhodan turned around. "Everyone leave his position. There's a small hangar on B-deck: go there immediately and get into the lifeboat spacer there. You've no time to lose!"

The last report Rhodan received was: "The Arkonide fleet has taken off, sir!"

He looked at the chronometer. Their headstart amounted to a matter of 12 minutes. If the *Lotus* had immediately understood the thrice repeated "Mercant", it could arrive in 5 or 6 minutes and take them on board, lifeboat and all. The newly developed frequency damper would prevent the *Lotus* from being spotted.

"Get going!" he ordered Maj. Ostal. "I'll get this ship ready by myself. Save a place for me in the lifeboat—of course the pilot's seat! See you soon, Major! You've done a good job!"

The compliment from the mouth of the Administrator of the Solar Imperium in this dangerous situation struck the Major as a bit odd. Had Rhodan said it because he knew that if the Regent's robotships arrived very soon he would never have another chance to say it?

Perry Rhodan had no time for such thoughts. The small Ekhonide ship raced at a speed that threatened to tear it apart, yet in spite of all its strain, it was slow in comparison to the ships of the Arkonide fleet.

But perhaps it was possible to shake off the pursuers in some other manner? And for the preparations for that, Rhodan allowed himself no time to think of other things.

He made an atomic bomb out of the ship!

His brain functioned as precisely as a positronicomputer.

A twist of a dial, a press of a button, a twist of another dial. And then he was ready.

The small transformer would explode first, in 2 or 3 minutes. Its explosion would detonate half a dozen energy storage banks and then the entire ship would be a blazing atomic inferno.

Now Perry Rhodan raced to the hangar on B-deck.

2 or 3 minutes remaining until the ship blew up—that span of time was considerably limited. But there was no other way out.

Maj. Ostal had saved him his seat.

With a reverberating cracking the inner hatch of the hangar closed, then the entrance hatch of the lifeboat was shut. Rhodan transmitted the electronic signal that triggered the opening of the outer hatch in the ship's hull.

Slowly—much too slowly—it started to open.

Finally the outer hatch had opened 1/3d of the way. Rhodan could wait no longer.

Engine thrust at 33% capacity! The small lifeboat engines pushed the tiny spacecraft, crammed with nearly 40 men, out into open space with only centimeters to spare on either side of the partially blocked hatchway.

They hurtled into the void. To the right shone the yellowish star Naral, glowing like the eye of a beast of prey. Somewhere behind them the robotspacers of the Arkonide Fleet were shooting towards them.

Perry Rhodan had sped the small lifeboat up to full speed. The little craft, first supplied with the velocity of its mothership and now well underway thanks to its relatively powerful engines, was not nearly out of the danger zone yet. Behind them the Ekhonide ship became a tiny sun swiftly expanding in all directions at once.

Over the large vidscreen in his office, Gen. Sutokk witnessed the destruction of the Ekhonide ship as relayed by cameras aboard one of the robotspacers.

His hard face twisted into a satisfied smile but it quickly gave way to an expression of regret. "Now I'll never find out which Springer clan was collaborating with these Terrans. That's too bad. But I won't tell the Regent that. I'll just say that the *Tigris* crew no longer exists . . ."

He was listening with only half an ear. Then it was announced that in spite of his orders to the contrary, ships were taking off. One of them had been the *Mab* 1 and he had been told nothing about it because of an unavoidable mixup in communications. As he listened to this piece of news, the *Mab* 1 was long vanished into the depths of the galaxy and could no longer be reached.

Gen. Sutokk could have been satisfied with the outcome of the operation, however, except when he remembered how unreasonable stupidly some of his people had suddenly acted, actions not even his scientists could explain. Then he came near to an outburst of rage.

Suddenly he remembered the captain of the *Tigris*. He was still with Egg-Or.

Why hadn't he been sent here yet?

"Get me Egg-Or!" Sutokk roared into the microphone. Egg-Or's face soon appeared on the vidscreen. "Egg-Or, did the stupidity epidemic hit you too? What's going on here on this planet all of a sudden? You mean to say you sent the captain over to see me . . . without any guards?! Oh, this is too much . . . !" At that point Gen. Sutokk got up and ran out of his office for some fresh air. His staff breathed easier, in relief.

No Arkonide ship spotted the *Lotus* when she sprang into the Naral System, took on a tiny lifeboat packed full with men and then disappeared in the direction of the Solar System once more. The newly developed frequency damper covered for any spring through hyperspace.

The danger that the Robot Regent might have discovered Earth's position after all still existed but only for the next 3 to 4 days. When the 4th day had passed, the danger was over. What Perry Rhodan had secretly feared had not materialized—no Arkonide spacespheres had appeared in Earth's skies!

All Terran ships were ordered to return. Only the few ships already equipped with the damper were allowed to make transitions. All the others had to wait until they too were supplied with the equipment that did not allow vibrations from the structocomp to escape into space. But so that the Robot Regent would not immediately learn that Terran ships were outfitted with an important new device, Perry Rhodan had some of his damper-equipped starships in the middle of the Galaxy make serial *undamped* transitions which of course would be detected by the Great Imperium's sensor stations. Perry Rhodan was well aware that he could not have his ships doing that for months on end, for if nothing else, he knew enough not to underestimate the Robot Regent. But every day he realized more & more that time worked for him and against Arkon.

Rhodan looked up from his desk.

Maj. Clyde Ostal stepped in. "Sir," he announced, "Professor Manoli has just informed me of the death of Mabdan 3. He died as a result of Arkonide forced hypnosis. There was nothing that could be done for him."

"And what about the old Mabdan . . . Mabdan 1: is he still lying in a drugged stupor?"

Clyde Ostal smiled. "That's why I asked to speak to you, sir . . . Mabdan 1 is waiting in the anteroom. He's in good health now and feeling fine. He wants to thank you for his rescue from his addiction. Our doctors did wonders with him."

"Then send him in, Ostal. After that, go remind Mr. Bell of the former drug smuggler on Ekhas and that the sum of money we owe him should be paid immediately. After all, who knows when we might need a friend . . . ?"

500 ADVENTURES FROM NOW
Life is hectic aboard the
Spaceship of the Possessed

THE SHIP OF THINGS TO COME

EXISTENCE QUESTIONABLE.

That is the question facing the 8000 exiles from Earth, banished to Grautier, 7th planet of the Myrtha system, lying far off the routes of the interstellar space lanes. For they have learned, these transplaneted Terrestrials, that they are not alone on their grave new world—in the mountains exists a semi-intelligent race of monkeys, the Mungos, and in the jungles of the lowland live strange blue dwarfs who are endowed with amazing paramechanical & parapsychological powers.

But that's not all.

There are also intelligent beings inhabiting the 12th planet of the system—the Whistlers—and their recent invasion of Grautier has made the continued existence of the colonists quite questionable.

To protect themselves against a potential second invasion, A group of Grautierians "reciprocate" the visit of the Whistlers, appearing on their planet in the guise of—

AMBASSADORS FROM AURIGEL
By
Kurt Mahr

Stop Press! Flash!

IT'S COMING!!!

1939: The First World Science Fiction Convention. Ray Bradbury, Ray Cummings, Forrest J Ackerman, Ross Rocklynne, Eando Binder, Sam Moskowitz, Willy Ley, Jack Williamson among the attendees.

1974: 40th Anniversary Celebration of the Los Angeles Science Fantasy Society; Ray Bradbury, Robert Bloch, Forrest J Ackerman, Ross Rocklynne, Larry Niven, Jerry Pournelle, Wendayne Ackerman, A. E. van Vogt, among those in attendance.

In between, the Chicon ('40), Denvention ('41), Pacificon ('46), regional Cons, Cons in England, Australia, Germany, Italy, Sweden, Japan, Canada, France, Spain and elsewhere; Star Trek Cons, Comicons, Mythicons, Filmcons, the Famous Monsters Con and so on & so on.

NOW . . . *are you ready for this???*

This Coming November:

THE RHOCON!

The Co-Creator of PERRY RHODAN, Walter Ernsting, is expected from Austria.

Forrest J & Wendayne Ackerman as well as Kris Dark-on will be flying in from Hollywood.

The American Publishers of PERRY RHODAN will be there.

And it wouldn't be complete without *Gray Morrow*.

The time: very likely Nov. 21, 22, 23.

The place: very probably Orlando, Florida.

The sponsor: super-Rhofan Tim Whalen who scored 100% correct on the First Rhodan Contest.

WATCH THIS SPACE! Every month from now on till Con Time there'll be more information about THE RHO-CON! Memberships available soon. Plan now to attend!

600 ADVENTURES FROM NOW
The Plot Deepens with
The Time Diver

Shock Short

Shockingly, the author omitted his or her name from their manuscript (or womanuscript). We pray to hear from the writer of this "first" called—

PREY
By
?

Those look like rain clouds coming up, thought Bors, glancing at the horizon. And not any too soon.

Picking his way carefully among the rocks, he mounted the hill. He was unencumbered for the hunt had not gone well. Unless the others had had better luck the village would have to settle for the dried winter rations, what little was left. Bors tried to tell himself that soon game would once more cover the plain now blackened with drought. "Just let it rain," he whispered up at the darkening clouds. "That's all we need."

Suddenly his attention was captured by a streak of light against the sky. It was moving so fast! Fascinated he watched it drop below the horizon. Then remembering, he shrugged and continued on his way.

10 minutes later, panting from his exertions, he paused to rest in the shadow of an overhanging rock. Wearily his eyes scanned the washed-out surface below him.

What was that? He stared down into the valley. "Something is moving down there—but what?" not knowing he had spoken. No longer tired, he crept through what little cover there was until at last he reached the edge of what was now desert.

Bors could see the prey better now as it moved from rock to rock. He watched avidly as it raised its head at the sound of the approaching rain. And he wondered at its strangeness and unfamiliarity. It was coming closer, working its way over to his place of concealment now. Soon it would be in easy reach, as his stomach vigorously reminded him. Well, hope it tastes better than it looks, he thought, with a slight revulsion.

Capt. Mason surveyed the emptiness about him and sighed. What a godforsaken place, he thought, as he reached for his communicator. Guess I'd better check in with the ship.

Suddenly he froze as he saw the monster lying in wait. For a moment 2 blue eyes stared into multi-lensed multicolored ones. Then with a yell, Mason reached for his gun even as 17-fingered claws ripped through his spacesuited body.

And the rains came at last to the black . . . and red . . . desert.

From the Burgeoning World of the Triplanetary Service
Comes—

NEW LENSMAN

By

William B. Ellern

PART 3

Synopsis of Part 1 & 2

Lt. Larry McQueen of the Solarian Patrol has revealed to the Board of Directors of Copernicus, an underground city on the moon, that the Solar System was being watched by unknown aliens suspected of aggressive intentions and that the Patrol was alerting major spaceports and upgrading Solar defenses.

After the meeting Ron Love, Mayor of Copernicus, explained to Dr. Ray Kelvin, Director of the Moorpark Research Center, and Larry that the real intent of the meeting was to determine if they had been infiltrated. Using lie detectors installed by the previous Mayor, he determined that John Griffin, Director of Facilities, was a probable traitor.

Larry made arrangements to upgrade Copernicus' defenses by installation of Rodebush-Bergenholm fields. This included cutting shock-insulating slots around the city and copper-plating the exposed surface.

Mayor Love examined the Central File computer's personnel records and found over 17 suspects. He turned the matter over to Col. Owen Hanovich, Director of Security. He also called in Rog Philips, an ex-employee of Facilities, to monitor that department's activities.

Larry met with Col. Hanovich, who recognized him as a Sector Chief of the Triplanetary Service. They discussed plans for watching the suspects. On the way back to his hotel, Larry was rendered unconscious and kidnapped.

Chapter 4

IN THE SANCTUARY

It was cold. Bitterly cold. Lt. Larry McQueen's first sensation as he woke up was that he was freezing. He was lying on a hard surface and there was cloth under his face. He tried to move his hands to roll over, and couldn't: They were bound behind him. Awake now, he tried to see, and couldn't. He blinked his eyes. He felt them blink. Darkness. He lay quietly awhile longer, trying to breathe normally. Listening. Silence. It was cold and no sound penetrated the darkness.

He pulled his feet up. They were bound together. He rolled over and worked himself into a sitting position. He tried to move his fingers. Stuck. He must be bound with some sort of adhesive tape. If he could just get his fingers loose or slip his shirt . . . No such luck. It was a workman-like job done by a professional. Larry struggled with it for awhile and then gave up.

"Hello," he said. The sound of his voice reverberated from the walls. He spoke several times trying to determine from the sound the size of the room. Small. Noisy. Metal walls? A spaceship maybe? But why so dark, so silent and so cold?

Larry was considering trying to explore the room when he heard the sound of footsteps. They were coming closer. He had time to resume his former position when there was the sound of a bar being removed and a door opening. Larry's dark-adapted eyes hurt when the light was turned on, even though he kept them closed, feigning unconsciousness.

"Our spacehound is still out, I see," a sneering voice said. Then apparently turning to someone else the man said, "Get in there! Over in the corner! Dump the food. You can turn on the heater when we leave. Durk, you watch her. I want to take a closer look at our other guest."

The footsteps came closer. A boot wacked into Larry's ribs. He was able to keep his eyes closed and only let out a little groan. The boot hooked under his shoulder and he was rolled over. "Pretty, isn't he?" came the voice again. The man stood over Larry for a moment and then Larry heard him turn.

"Ah, yes. One thing more before we leave." The footsteps moved to another part of the room. "Give me your blouse." There was a shocked silence. The voice repeated the demand. There was another silence and then the sound of scuffling and the ripping of cloth. A choked protest. The sound of someone being slapped and falling down. More cloth ripping.

The men left. There were the sounds of a bar being dropped into place and of footsteps dying away. Now there was only the soft sound of a woman crying.

Larry opened his eyes. They had adjusted to the bright light now. In the corner of what appeared to be a public washroom was a girl huddled in a little heap, crying. Larry must have made some kind of noise because she suddenly looked up at him. She was beautiful in spite of the tear-stained cheeks. She had red hair, young; about 20 or so, Larry guessed. She wore slacks, a bra and the remnants of a blouse. The red mark where she had been slapped was beginning to show on her face.

"Hello," Larry said.

She looked at Larry for a moment and then went back to crying. Her hands covering her face.

Larry waited. The tiles were cold and he could see his breath. He sat up again. The room was a tiled restroom. That explained the echo. Larry's boots were gone, as were his belt, money belt, helmet and goggles, his dress jacket and, so far as he could tell, the contents of his pockets. His shirt buttons and collar stays were still present, he noted. That would help.

A few moments later the sobbing had abated to almost nothing. The girl was beginning to shiver a little.

"Could you get that heater going?" Larry asked. "It's awful cold in here."

There was a moment's pause. Then the girl got up and stumbled over to the heater. She turned on the switch. Nothing happened.

"You have to plug it in," Larry said, trying to keep his voice as sympathetic as possible. "The outlet is in the wall over there." Larry nodded in the direction of the outlet.

The girl moved the heater and plugged it in. Almost immediately Larry could feel the radiant heat.

"Better?" Larry asked.

The girl nodded.

"Anything I can do to help?"

The girl shook her head.

"Name?"

She didn't answer but just looked at him. It was as if she couldn't remember, or wouldn't remember, or couldn't believe that she was really here.

"What's your name?" Larry prompted again.

"Pamela," she said in a very small voice.

"Alright, Pamela," Larry said. "I'd like you to do something special for me."

She nodded.

"Go over and touch the wall."

She obeyed him.

"Now the sink . . . a faucet . . . the wall again . . . now stomp on the floor. Look around the room. Do you see anything you like?"

She nodded, "The heater."

"Good. Go over to it. Look at it. Touch it. Feel its warmth. Try to sense it as much as possible. OK?"

Pamela followed his directions.

"Alright, now how do you feel?"

"Better."

"Good!" Larry said. "That was an exercise in being right here, right now. A schoolmate of mine taught it to me."

"You're tied up."

"Let's say that I get wrapped up in my work," Larry said with a broad smile. "I'd offer you my shirt except that, looks to the contrary, this is a one-piece jumper."

"Oh!" Pamela looked down and then tried to cover herself with her arms. "I'm sorry, I . . ."

"It's alright. I'm sure that you have at least one bathing suit that's more revealing. Besides, a beautiful girl should show off her charms."

She looked at Larry and smiled. A startling effect on a beautiful, tear-stained face.

"You're right, of course," she said, and hesitatingly dropped her arms. "I can't very well go around all the time like this. Can I unwrap you?"

"If you're sure I won't r-r-r-ravish you," he said with a broad smile. It was a quote from a recent hit comedy show. She laughed.

"Silly," she called him.

It didn't taken long to unwrap the tape from around

Larry's arms. He winced as the last of it came off and his arms dropped to his side.

Pamela noticed and asked what was wrong. Larry explained through gritted teeth that his arms were numb and the shoulder muscles cramped from the long period he had been bound. Pamela stripped the tape from his legs and then made him lie down on the blanket while she massaged his back. Before long the needles of pain had left his arms and the soreness was gone from his back. He stopped her, rolled over and looked up at her kneeling next to him. He squelched the little thought that said "D cup" and tried to think of something encouraging to say to her. Whether it was that he was distracted by her beauty or because there was nothing encouraging to be said, Larry couldn't tell, but the words didn't come. So he just looked at her for awhile.

"What's your name?" she asked, finally breaking the silence.

"Larry McQueen, Lieutenant, Solarian Patrol," he answered. "I could give you my serial number but that wouldn't mean much. Where are we?"

"I don't know for sure but by the looks of things we're in the Sanctuary," she said. Seeing the blank look on Larry's face, she explained. "The Sanctuary's a meteor shelter built about a mile underneath the Dome. I was 9 the last time I was down here. It was sealed off after the last war. I'm sure that's where we are."

"How did we get down here?"

"There are elevators at the south end of the Dome."

"Any idea why you're here?" Larry asked.

"Kidnapping?" she shrugged. "I doubt that my father has enough money to make it worth their while."

"Who's your father? You didn't tell me your last name."

"Johnstone," she said. "My father is Ted Johnstone, the Director of Copernicus Control."

Larry made no comment but things fell together in his mind with an almost audible click. Pamela Johnstone was being held for ransom alright, but it was very doubtful that the ransom price was money. More likely pressure was being secretly put on her father. The ransom price was probably access to, if not actual control of, the operations of Copernicus Control. Larry ventured to guess that they would never willingly release Pamela. If they did, they would lose their hold over the Director of Copernicus Control. They had to keep her alive but that didn't mean that they couldn't use her while she was being held. So they roughed her up, tore off part of her clothes and threw her in with another prisoner, from whom they wanted some information. They expected him to comfort, calm and get involved with her. Larry looked at Pamela. Yes, that would be real easy to do. And once he was caught in that trap, they would tell him that he had to spill everything he knew or they would skin her alive. If Johnstone didn't cooperate or if they were close to the actual attack, they would probably do just that to her, too. If he played it cool, but interested, they might have more time than if he either rejected her or was obviously enamored. He also had a good idea of what both of their fates would be if they didn't escape.

"Let's see what they left us to eat," he said, getting up and going over to the box of containers that Pamela and one of the guards had brought. He estimated that there was enough food for about five days. More if they rationed it out.

"Any idea what day it is?" Larry asked.

"No."

"It looks like we're going to spend the next couple of days here, all alone, together, in our secret hideaway. Unless . . . how is the door locked?" Larry asked.

"There's a bar across it."

"Does the bar slide back?"

"Yes, I think so."

"Close your eyes and try to visualize it. How big is it and where is it on the door?"

Pamela indicated the size of the bar and then, standing in front of him, showed Larry the location on the door.

Larry noticed a gentle lilac perfume about her hair and then brought himself up sternly.

"I'm hungry, how about you?" he said.

She nodded.

"Would you get us some food while I check to see if there might be some other sort of exit to this room?"

She smiled at him and Larry gave a quick smile back.

Larry started at one side of the door into the room and worked his way completely around it to the other side of the door, searching not for an exit but a bug or a "snoop", as the miniature television cameras are called. He found two tiles which had apparently been removed and replaced. The grout around them was of a slightly different shade than that of the rest of the wall. He examined the tiles closely before moving past them and found a little shiny spot on each. Larry suspected that behind each was a snoop and possibly a contact microphone. Up in a corner of the room was something that looked for all the world like a spider web, except what would a spider be doing down here? Larry went over the ceiling as best he could. He concluded that unless they had repainted or done a better job of color matching than on the tiles, nothing had been installed from his side.

"Is the Sanctuary a single level high or are there several levels to it?" he asked Pamela.

"I think it's about five or six levels high," she said.

"Well, the only way out seems to be the door," Larry said, and then sat down next to Pamela. From this point on his escaping depended upon whether she was really the person she said she was. It was going to be interesting finding out.

* * *

Things were moving fast out on the surface of the crater and in the Moorpark Research Center. Dr. Kelvin had organized his Project Hard Hat team and the team had mobilized over half of the research center's personnel and facilities; which group was in turn getting ready to take over the rest of the research center, as well as part of Copernicus Control. The blaster batteries over the city had been dismantled and preparations were being made to install them at new sites farther around the rim. Until the sites were ready, the projectors were being put to other uses. Three had been mounted in a triangle aboard one of the center's four mobile laboratory spaceships. They were being adjusted to produce a 100-foot circle of intense heat to melt the crusty, gravel-like material of the surface of Copernicus into a smooth, glassy sheet that could be evenly plated with a continuous evaporative coating of copper. The second laboratory spaceship was being outfitted to provide that coating, or rather it was being chopped up, since, outfitting consisted of cutting away considerable portions of the hull, installing bracing, a small blaster for heating and ion focusing fields to direct the flow of gaseous copper as it was evaporated from the surface of the yet to be delivered ingot.

Dr. Kelvin himself was sitting in his office in the research center looking at what appeared to be a model of an oil derrick loaded with equipment.

"OK, what have you got?" he asked of the two engineers who had brought the model into his office.

"This is a model of the 'slot cutter'," one engineer explained. "It represents a 60-foot tower of composition ceramo-steel. It's faced with wall shields and three courses of polycyclic screens. The legs are anc' ored with tractors, one mounted on each leg pointing downward into the rock underneath the tower. In a line up the side of the tower facing the crater wall are seven blasters, from the battery we just dismantled. At the bottom of the stack of blasters, and in the space between each blaster, is mounted a tractor beam. The whole assembly of blasters and tractors can be rotated up and down by remote control. This makes it possible to cut a slot, instead of a series of holes, in the wall of the crater.

"The purpose of the tractors is to remove the material as fast as it is softened, rather than having to wait until it is vaporized. If the material could be removed from the direct beam fast enough, it would be possible to cut a six-foot hole in the rock at 100 feet per second with these projectors as deep as we wish. We think with proper timing of the movement of the array, we can approach that rate. The spacing of the beams is three feet, with the beams themselves an oval of about six by eight feet. The molten rock will be pulled out of the slot at a rate of over 4500 cubic feet per second. At this rate it will take about 21 days to cut the larger of the two slots.

"Here is a computer simulation of the problem and our solution." The engineer handed Dr. Kelvin a reel of tape.

Dr. Kelvin weighed the tape in his hand for a moment. Based on what he had already seen, he was contemplating whether to ask his questions and give his lecture now or to wait until after the reel of tape had been run on the computer. He decided to run the tape. He dropped it into the player and watched the drafting tank opposite his desk as a computer simulated model of the tower cut a slot in a computer simulated model of the crater wall. Stresses, flow rates, safety margins and the like were shown. At the conclusion of the tape Dr. Kelvin leaned back in his chair a moment before saying anything.

"*I do not like it!*" he said slowly, with careful emphasis. Both engineers visibly blanched. "I don't like the philosophy behind the method and I don't like the method it produced.

"Less than four days from now the surface smoothing will be complete," he continued. "In another three and a half days from then the coating operation on that surface will be complete. At the end of that time I want to be ready to go right into plating the slots. That means that by the time you are started, there will be six to seven days left to complete cutting a slot about six feet wide and up to two miles deep around Copernicus.

"For obvious reasons . . ." Dr. Kelvin shrugged, and started again. "Because no one has worked out a way to rapidly remove material from the slot on the far side, we've gone from a rectangular area around Copernicus to a triangular area for the top surface. But the job remains big. So big that five years ago it would have been beyond our capability. The amount of material to be removed is in excess of 15 *billion* cubic feet! That is now within our present capacity and we *will* do it *rapidly!*

"There are two ways to approach any new problem.

The first, and unfortunately the most common way, is to use brute force. Brute force is always expensive. It eats up power and time. It wastes material and resources. It's only used because the problem is not properly defined, because of tradition, or because someone has not taken the time to find a better solution.

"The second way of approaching a problem can be summarized in one word, 'sneakiness'. I like that word because it's descriptive of the main characteristics of this method. When someone else sees this type of solution to a problem for the firstime, they think, 'How neat! What a sneaky way to do it! Why didn't I think of that?' A sneaky method does things with a minimum of flare and noise and there is invariably a usable by-product as a bonus.

"With this in mind, let's take a look at your solution," Dr. Kelvin said. "It's obviously a brute force solution. You're going to have a circus that can be seen with the naked eye all the way to Tellus. This whole sector of moonscape is going to be covered with blown out magma and gasses. When the job is done half of the crater will be ankle deep in hot lava.

"Now I confess that I've been considering the problem I gave you ever since I gave it to you. There is a better way.

"First let's redefine the basic problem in terms of the function involved. The problem is not to 'cut a slot'. The problem is to 'remove material'. To remove, for example, a slab of material 37½ miles long, two miles high and six feet thick. The first step, I think, is for you gentlemen to determine how much of that slab you can handle at one time, and the method of handling it, and then to plan to cut it into sizes accordingly."

Dr. Kelvin was pleased to notice that as he spoke a

look of comprehension was beginning to appear in the engineers' faces. They were beginning to see a solution that had been staring them in the face.

"If you use a very thin, fan-shaped beam to cut the slabs, the lava and gasses can be used to act as a lubricant for sliding the slabs out. Since the slabs will be flat sided, you won't have the erosion problems inherent with the bulk removal of hot lava and gasses, which you didn't taken into account in your calculations for your simulation. Finally, I have a use for the slabs. That needn't concern you now, however. I'll expect to see an analysis in detail of this method the first thing tomorrow. Thank you."

Dr. Kelvin ushered the two engineers out of his office and spent a few minutes on a bit of analysis of the optimum angle to the perpendicular to make the slot, taking into account the coriolis force. A quick approximation showed it to be too small to be of significance.

* * *

In the next two days considerable progress was made. The laboratory spaceship that had been reworked into a "smoother" had processed over half of the surface covering Copernicus. Work on the spaceship to do the coating had stopped because of a higher priority on the conversion of the remaining two laboratory spaceships into slot cutters.

The "oil derrick" idea was abandoned. Instead, tractor beams capable of anchoring the spaceships while sliding out slabs 500 feet on a side were being mounted. Blasters, capable of producing incredibly powerful, inch-thick, fan-shaped beams were being mounted outside the tractors, to cut the slabs. Bracing for the whole ship was being added with a lavish hand and so thickly it was almost impossible to get to the equipment afterwards. One humorist in the crew commented that the greatest danger in manning a tractor ship was trying to get out after you had eaten your lunch, to which another commented that one more "I" beam and even death would not release you. It was a tight fit.

The first slot cutter was tested by cutting a series of holes two miles deep every 500 feet along the path of the longest slot. Then, after a short period of experimentation with technique, and modification with cutters and torch, the slabs were sliding out and down the crater wall like logs down a sluice-way. At the bottom of the wall they were allowed to fall flat and slide out onto the crater floor in long, orderly rows.

The second slot cutter would be complete and working by midnight. Dr. Kelvin's original schedule couldn't be met. The blocks couldn't be cut and slid out that fast without breaking or jamming in the slot, but they could do better than the original estimate of 21 days. Much better!

In the eastern corner of the triangle covering the city of Copernicus the first of three new areas were being cut into the rock with mining machines. These were to house the field generators when they arrived.

This was another matter.

"Where in hell are my field generators?" Dr. Kelvin snarled at the man on the plate.

George Smith, a top official of Tellus Electric, looked blankly back at Dr. Kelvin. "I don't know," he said tiredly. "Where about in hell did you leave them?"

Dr. Kelvin glared at the man, then realized what he had said and struggled to keep a straight face. He chuckled. The man on the plate just looked tired.

"Alright, I'm looking for the Rodebush-Bergenholm field generators your company was contractually committed to deliver to the New York Spaceport eight hours ago."

"I have 16 generators sitting on the floor now. They are coming off my production line at a rate of one every two hours. They're costing me 100 credits an hour each for each hour they stand there. Not one is working."

Dr. Kelvin hesitated for a moment, then said, "Alright, I would like to help you out. If you'll turn on your recorder, I'll make you a proposal."

"It's on."

"I propose that you crate up the next three generators that come off of your production line and send them to me, along with six full sets of prints and an engineer familiar with the generator. When you get the first few working, you'll be able to tell your engineer what mistakes were made in the production line and he can fix them here. If parts are needed and we don't have them in stock, we have the facilities to fabricate them just as fast as you could. If additional troubleshooting is needed, we'll let your man supervise and charge you for the people and material used at our going rate plus 300% overhead. This saves you the cost of transportation time after the generators are working and gets the generator to us faster. Our acceptance of the generator is then dependent on when it's working properly, not on when it arrives. That's the end of my proposal."

"That sounds good, except your overhead rate is too high."

"You can send all your own people," Dr. Kelvin answered. "300% wouldn't even touch their transportation costs, but . . ."

"How about the troubleshooting manpower you have available. How many and what kind of people do you have?"

"I can guarantee you up to 10 technicians and two engineers within 20 minutes of your requirements," he said, thinking of two particular engineers he'd assign.

Agreement was reached. The tapes were witnessed and sealed.

A few minutes later Dr. Kelvin was again on the visiphone. This time to an Earthside transportation company.

"Were in hell is my copper?" he snarled at the man on the plate.

* * *

Hanovich had organized his teams too late to catch the kidnapping of either Lt. McQueen or Pamela Johnstone. At the moment the team watching the suspects saw only people going about their normal affairs, minding their own business and in general being model citizens. The two teams checking personal records had come a long way without success. There had been no indication that any suspect had purchased extra food or even any unusual items. The customs records indicated that nothing out of the ordinary had been brought in. A survey of the suspects' present personal effects had been made with one team entering a suspect's empty apartment and temporarily turning off spy-ray blocks, while the other sat at a spy-ray installation in Security and photographed the contents of drawers, closets, cabinets, etc., which had been covered by the blocks. Nothing even mildly interesting was found. A professional rarely makes this kind of mistake. It was noted that the apartments were spartan in the lack of knick-knacks and souvenirs that everyone seems to accumulate.

The teams finally started through the records of the agencies in which the suspects worked. The purpose was to see if, and how, the agencies had been used. Indeed, they had! A large amount of equipment had been requisitioned out of the Facilities Stores. It was then apparent, in retrospect, why nothing had been brought in or purchased. A statistical check was made on the food consumed by the hospital, where three suspects worked, against the number of staff members and patients. A high probability was established that this was the source of food for the missing suspects.

Judge Fox had issued search warrants on his request but unless he came up with something solid soon to justify the Judge's trust, things were going to get sticky.

The numbers that characters in this story throw off so casually are converted from the metric system for the American reader's convenience. In most cases calculations consist of single whole number multiplications, or simple decimal point shifts—simple in the metric system where everything is in powers of 10—difficult in the (ex-) English system with its 12 inch feet and 5280 foot miles. WBE.

Shock Short

From the Author of "Alien Carnival" & "Mama Hates Green" you expect a Special Kind of Story. You will not be disappointed in—

A SPECIAL KIND OF FLOWER

By Walt Liebscher

For all of his 6 years on this Earth Lonny Dempster had lived a normal, happy life. Now it was the time of changes and his life would nevermore be the same.

A week before he was to enter the first grade of the township school his mother took him on her lap, nestled his curly head against her bosom and gently rocked back & forth.

"How's Mommy's little boy today?"

"Fine, Mom, just fine."

"Can you keep a big, big secret?" She kept on rocking.

"If it's for you, Mom, I can."

She marvelled at the sound of his voice, like a highly honed alto flute, mellow and pure.

"Mom's going to tell you a lot of things that, at first, you will have trouble understanding. But, as time goes on, you will accept these things, and learn to cope with them. Now listen real hard. OK?"

"OK. Mom."

Then she told him of how a huge silver ship, from a far away star, had landed on Earth. Of how the people

144

on this ship were different from Earthmen, gifted with powers of the mind far beyond anything he had ever experienced. They could rise off the ground, instantly remember any printed page, move objects just by thinking, and of a few very special chosen ones who could mentally draw in matter from the air, sea and land and produce objects seemingly out of thin air.

She then explained to him why it was necessary to hide all of these gifts, of how the people on Earth were intolerant of differentness and finally that she, his Mom, and his Daddy had been on that ship and that he, Lonny Dempster, would have these gifts. She concluded with the repeated warning that no one, except for those on a list she would give him, was ever to know about these powers, nor were they to be used in public. Then, for awhile, she was silent and a bit frightened, rocking back & forth, back & forth.

She took his little hands and pressed them hard against her temples. "Now, my sweet one," she said, "I want you to clear your mind and don't think of anything."

He did as she asked and almost immediately felt the flow of it, the warmth of it, the sheer wonder of it. He had the gifts.

The next few weeks were pure joy for Lonny. In the privacy of his room he would rise up and fly around, he practiced moving his toys at will, he made music on his toy piano from across the room.

School was easy, as his mother said it would be, and he was becoming used to hiding his talents. And he liked the other kids his mother said he could play with, the ones like himself, especially a little girl named Suzie Colvin.

Then, slowly but surely, he felt it all began to slip away. He still knew what people were thinking but no longer could he elevate, or play his piano, or move things. The sadness began.

School became a nightmare. He had to study pages over & over again. He just couldn't remember. The other boys and girls like himself began to avoid his company and he felt terribly alone.

One day Suzie found him sitting on a bench in the far corner of the playerground. "What's the matter, Lonny?" she asked. "You look real sad."

He looked at her, reaching out. "I'm scared, Suzie, I'm scared. I think I've lost the gifts."

"Are you sure? All of them?"

"All except the mind thing. I can still tell what the other ones are thinking. But I can't raise up, or move my toys, or any of those things."

"Gosh, that's awful," Suzie said. "But you can still block. I can't read you."

"I guess that's something," he said dejectedly.

"Maybe if you opened up for me it would help. Want to try?"

"You won't like it."

"But I'm your best friend and I'm not afraid. Maybe I can help. Anyway let's try."

He took hold of her hand, pressed hard and looked straight into her eyes. Then he released the block and let her slip in.

Almost immediately she recoiled in horror. Then she caught hold of herself and gazed into his eyes. Tear after tear after tear rolled down her cheeks as she was immersed in silent torment and stifling loneliness. But there was something, something strange and illusive that was almost blotted out by the ocean of tears inside him.

After awhile she withdrew and sat silent and sad.

"I told you you wouldn't like it," he said.

"Oh, Lonny, my poor Lonny, how dreadful. It's bad and I don't know how to help. Have you told your Mom?"

"I'm afraid."

"Afraid of your Mom?"

"Oh, not that way. I know she loves me but I think I'm some kind of a freak, like in the circus, and I don't want her to know."

"Oh, Lonny, how terrible. But she's the only one who can help, I think. You've just got to tell her."

"I guess you're right. Thanks, Suzie." He got up and ambled slowly into the woods next to the playground.

She started to say something but couldn't think of anything. And she wondered about that strange, puzzling, unknown power she had sensed in the back of his mind. Somehow she had to find out what it was. She was sure it was important, very important.

His mother knew something was troubling him. She also knew he would seek her out when the time came. He was an unusual one, her son, a loner, and she sensed he would never be really content or at peace. But she must be careful not to let him know she knew, and not be overly protective.

"Can we talk, Mom?"

"Sure, son, something bothering you?"

"I suppose. Let's go out and sit in the swing. OK?"

"If that's what you want, sweets." She followed him out to the arbor.

"Mom, will you always love me, no matter what?"

He's hurting and he's very vulnerable, she thought. Be very careful. "Always, son, no matter what, and don't you ever doubt it." She gave him a big bear hug. "You're Mom's little treasure and you always will be."

For a long moment he basked in the warmth of her embrace. "Mom, I don't want you to hate me but I can't help it."

That hurt and she fought back a welling of tears. Take hold. "Oh, son, no matter what it is that's bothering you, no matter what, I could never even begin to hate you. How could you even think of such a thing?" One tear did manage to slip through.

"Because I'm different."

"Different? How?" She squeezed his hand to reassure him.

He drew in a deep breath and gave a long sigh. "I'm a freak. I've lost the gifts."

She was stunned. Great God, not that, she thought. He's a blind one. He really is a freak. What can I tell him?

Too late she realized that, in her confusion, she had unblocked. He knew. She looked down at his pitiful, searching countenance. The tears were flowing freely. There was nothing she could do. Nothing.

"I'm sorry, Mom, really sorry." He slipped his hands from hers and walked away.

She made no attempt to stop him. He had to work it out for himself. Then she broke down and wept uncontrollably.

"Lonny is a lunkhead, Lonny is a lunkhead, can't move a stone or rise above his bedstead."

They had him in the center of a circle and, with joined hands, were skipping around him. He just stood there, half hearing, deep in hurt. He couldn't fight back. He had nothing to fight with. He was incapable of hate. In a strange way, he felt sorry for his tormentors.

"Stop it, you mean kids, stop it," said Suzie Colvin. "Leave him alone."

"Oh, go 'way, Suzie, and leave us alone."

"I won't. Besides he's better than you are. He's special."

"Ha," said one of the boys. "I'd like to see him prove it."

She walked towards Lonny and they broke the circle for her. She took his hands in hers and stared deep into his eyes.

"Lonny," she said, "listen to me. You are special. I figured it out. Think, Lonny, think real hard. Hold out your hand and think. Think—think flowers."

He held out his hand. "Think flowers, Lonny, think and make a rose."

He began to feel the flow, the power. He concentrated deeply. Suddenly, from nowhere, a deep, red rosebud appeared in his hand. For the firsttime in months, he smiled. The others stared at him in stunned silence.

"See, Lonny, you can do it. You are better than they are." She threw her arms around him and gave him a big hug. "Make another, Lonny, you can do it. You're one of the special ones."

Again he held out his hand and concentrated. He produced a flower so big, so ravishing in its beauty, the others gasped with sheer astonishment. Then he slowly turned, looking at each one in turn, and walked out of the circle. "Thank you, Suzie. Thank you so very, very much."

She stood there, the huge flower resting against her tear-laden cheek. Behind him, as he walked, he was leaving a trail of flower petals.

The next morning the townspeople were astounded to find every surface street in the township inundated with flower blossoms. They found him at the end of Main Street, lying on the only bare spot. Death had frozen his face into a radiant smile.

Everyone for miles around attended the funeral. Some of the parents were reluctant but all of the children had insisted on being there.

When the services were over and everyone had left, a lonely little girl walked slowly up to the grave.

"They will never understand, Lonny," said Suzie Colvin. "It would have been very bad, having the special gift and none of the others. But I've got them all, Lonny, I really have, thanks to you, and I will miss you so very much."

Then she held out her little hands and thousands of lustrous petals dripped from her fingers, mingling with the flowers on the grave.

Several days later, when the caretaker came to clean up the grave, he was amazed at the color and size of a still fresh-looking rosebud in the center of the other drying flowers. He reached down to touch it to see if it was real. It was.

Then he shrugged his shoulders, shoveled everything into a wheelbarrow and pushed it towards the incinerator.

Had he taken the time to examine the bright, metallic-looking petals scattered throughout the flowers, he would have found them to be pure gold.

The Rhodanary

A Glossary of Words, Terms & Names
from the Universe of the Peacelord

Myra 4 (pronounced *my*-ruh): A cold deserted planet circling a dying sun 800 light-years from Earth. (See GALACTIC ALARM)

Venusian worm: A gigantic thing resembling an earthworm, living in symbiosis with large stick-like insects. (BASE ON VENUS, #4)

Helakar (rhymes with hell-a-car): City on Ferrol.

Antineutron screen: It cancels radiation. In THE RADIANT DOME Thora used it to envelop the whole Earth.

Decrystallization field: Arkonide device which loosens atomic binding force in crystalline structures, including metal. (GALACTIC ALARM)

Khelar-Het (rhymes with *key*-bar bet): Largest city on the Great Ocean Isthmus of Ferrol. (MUTANTS IN ACTION, #5)

The Solitude Intelligence: A unisexual nonhumanoid creature inhabiting an unusually silent planet.

Solitude: A planet in the dimension of the Druufs with the appearance of a Paradise (broad grasslands, small rivers and streams, parklike forests) but pervaded by an odor reminiscent of brimstone (atmosphere 1% hydrogen sulphide). Planet's diameter: 6820 miles. Surface gravity 1.12 normal. Atmosphere: nitrogen 60%, oxygen 35%, argon 4% . . . plus the unfortunate hydrogen sulphide, making the air malodorous. Daily rotation on axis: 18 hours and a few minutes. A green world with an unstable orbit. (DIMENSION SEARCH, #60)

CALLING The Series "real grundle, in the good sense" and signing himself "your mikoa", which, if we recall correctly, means "friend" in one of those languages out there in the Cosmos, KEVIN HENNESSEY briefly comments from Cornwall-on-Hudson, NY:

I enjoyed that surprise quiz you gave us in #54 (THE BLUE DWARFS) and I found it quite easy and that may be because I just finished #1 thru #34 over again. Boy, that must have taken me about two months to do.

JAMES RUDD of 3027 Caldwallader-sonk (which really zonks our mind if that's an actual street address), Cortland/OH 44410, has been with Perry since his 10th adventure and tells us:

I cannot understand how all these letters that are sent in and just criticize this great series. I am just 14 but I have read "Doc" Smith's Skylark and Lensmen, Heinlein, Asimov, Burroughs' Tarzan (all 24), John Carter of Mars, Venus, Perpendicular, Moon, Ray Bradbury, Orwell's 1984, and many more. Not to take away from these authors, they are all great, but Rhodan beat even these great books. Doc Savage and Capt. Future were great and I was surprised when I found out how good this series is. It is much better than either of these.

I don't think it would be a good idea to put out editions 100 or 200 in advance. It would spoil some of the suspense. And don't say "Just don't buy them", because any fan will buy any PR book out.

Atlan is a very interesting character. It would be a good idea to carry his series separately. (*WATCH FOR A MARVELOUS ANNOUNCEMENT SOON!*)

Please carry more of the "Great Rhodan Quiz". I scored a 94.

You now have Burroughs Posters so when do the PR posters come out? (*As soon as Jane has soothed Tarzan's jungled nerves.*)

Also, who comes up with the slang of the future? It is not very good. It might be better if it was stopped. (*You sure know how to brainpain a jak! In this case an Ack. That's future slang for "hurt a guy". Anybody else dislike the neological coinages?*)

"The Cat & the Canaries" was the berries—the razzberries. KEITH THOMPKINS . . . Helen Urban's Shock Short ("Cat & Canaries") was the cat's meow. ALICIA ARIA . . . Hooray, I just found out I'm human, because, like you said, my heart bled (blood *is* green with orange stripes, isn't it?) for "The Fate of the Neptunians". I'll hate to see COSMOS come to an end—you'll have to have some serial to follow it up! CHARLES STAHLMASTER . . . The Editor's "Résumé of Rays" was, er, colorful. CHESTER CORCORAN . . . "Replacement Part" should have been replaced by another Shock Short, it wasn't all that shocking. DENNIS MALLORY . . . "Replacement Part" was a good followup for Greg Akers' "Sizable Error". By the way, have you noticed how many Akers are writing science fiction? I think there are 3. GERROLD JOHNSON . . . I agreed with

Hector Pessina's philosophy in his review of TV's "Love War", that future man should be ruled by logic and not sentiment. And I'm not even a distant relative of Mr. Spock! FRANK ARNHEIM . . . Try and get more scientifilm reviews by Walt Liebscher, his review of "Dark Star" was just right. JERRY BECK . . . After reading "To Serf Man" I was, you should excuse the expression, surfeited with puns. LARRY NOVAK . . . Did anyone notice at the top of some of the pages in SPYBOT! that the Spybot! turned out as Skybot!? JIM BLACK. (*Only just about everybotty, Jim!*)

VICTOR T. WOODWARD of 437 Hyde St. Box 22, San Franciso/CA 94109, who has been reading science fiction for almost 20 years, says:

Your series has really captured me. I was beginning to think that Science Fiction was becoming a thing of the past the way most Science Fiction Authors write any more.

Letters intended for this dept.
should be addressed to:

FJA: THE PERRYSCOPE
2495 Glendower Ave.
Hollywood/CA 90027

PERRY'S A WINNER—ARE YOU?

"I just received a postcard about my winning the double sub," writes subscriber LINDA HAMER. "Thank you very much. I just love Perry Rhodan books in fact it is the only one I read, science fiction that is. I have the whole series from Book #1 plumb up to 54. They are all great. Thank you again for choosing me as your September winner. I never won anything before."

YOU could be the author of a similar letter.

Each month, one subscriber is picked to have his or her subscription *doubled*. This month it's JAMES L. JACKSON of Athens/GA who sent for 6 numbers—gets 12!

Send $6.75 now for the next 6 numbers of PERRY RHODAN or $11.25 for the next 10 numbers. Temporarily, subscriptions are not being accepted for more than 10 issues. (This does not mean PR is in any danger of being discontinued after that time—QUITE THE CONTRARY!)

Checks or money orders (write nothing on the back) to:

KRIS DARKON
2495 Glendower Ave.
Hollywood/CA 90027

PERRY RHODAN #64 thru

NAME ....

AGE ....

ADDRESS ....

CITY ....

STATE (Spell Out) ....

ZIP ....

COUNTRY ....

PERRY RHODAN

TESTING THE ROBOT REGENT

THE SOLAR SECURITY SERVICE: 32 of its best men, picked for a Special Action against the Positronicon of Arkon, the Robot Brain whose extent of dangerous knowledge must be ascertained by Perry Rhodan.

Can the Positronicon measure the frequencies emitted by the structocomps of hypertransing ships of the Solar Imperium? If so, there's danger to the Earth!

Maj. Clyde Ostal, in the year 2042, receives orders from the Peacelord himself to take over the armed spacer *Tigris* in order to test the Robot Regent.

At the same time, events on Grautier, the Exile planet, have gotten out of hand and are careening inexorably toward a catastrophic climax as—